RAWLSIAN EXPLORATIONS IN RELIGION
AND APPLIED PHILOSOPHY

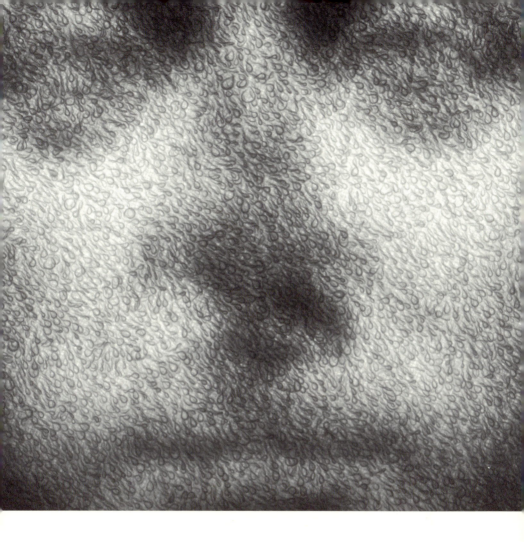

RAWLSIAN EXPLORATIONS IN RELIGION AND APPLIED PHILOSOPHY

DANIEL A. DOMBROWSKI

THE PENNSYLVANIA STATE UNIVERSITY PRESS
UNIVERSITY PARK, PENNSYLVANIA

An earlier version of parts of chapter 2 appeared as
"Rawls and War," *International Journal of Applied Phi-
losophy* 16 (2002): 185–200. An earlier version of parts
of chapter 5 appeared as "'All for the Greater Glory of
God': Was St. Ignatius Irrational?"
Logos 9 (2006): 109–17.

Library of Congress Cataloging-in-Publication Data

Dombrowski, Daniel A.
Rawlsian explorations in religion and applied philosophy / Daniel A. Dombrowski.
p. cm.
Summary: "Explores the political philosophy of John Rawls in relation to public policy issues,
including war, mental disability, nonhuman animals, legacy, and affirmative action. Pays
special attention to the relationship of religion to these issues and to the processual
characteristics of Rawls's method"—Provided by publisher.
Includes bibliographical references (p.) and index.
ISBN 978-0-271-04873-4 (cloth : alk. paper)
1. Policy sciences—Moral and ethical aspects.
2. Political science—Philosophy.
3. Religion and politics.
4. Rawls, John, 1921–2002.
5. Rawls, John, 1921–2002—Religion.
I. Title.

H97.D64 2011
320.092—dc22
2011002909

It is the policy of The Pennsylvania State University
Press to use acid-free paper. Publications on uncoated
stock satisfy the minimum requirements of American
National Standard for Information Sciences—Per-
manence of Paper for Printed Library Material,
ANSI Z39.48-1992.

The Pennsylvania State University Press is a member
of the Association of American University Presses.

This book is printed on Natures Natural, which
contains 50% post-consumer waste.

CONTENTS

PREFACE

One of the most common criticisms of John Rawls's political philosophy is that it is "too abstract." Sometimes this criticism is leveled against Rawls by those who lack the time or training to work through his admittedly difficult writings. But at other times it is used by scholars who are bothered by the distance between Rawlsian theory and the actual political world in which we live. As one colleague, after reading Rawls carefully, put it, one does not know how to get from "here" to "there" in Rawls, "there" being the realistic utopia that Rawls had in mind.

Admittedly, there are very good reasons why Rawls's thought is so abstract. In order to deal with the questions that were central to *A Theory of Justice*, Rawls was led to social contract theory, but only to a version that was raised to a higher level of abstraction than that found in traditional social contract theorists (Rawls 1996, xvii). This need for a greater degree of abstraction is amplified in his later writings, wherein citizens are seen to differ, sometimes uncompromisingly so, in the comprehensive doctrines that they are willing to affirm (which are very often religious in character), such that the differences themselves generate the process of abstraction so as to achieve the higher ground that is required to understand what a just society (or a just international order) would be like. That is, by abstracting from the social world we are able "to gain a clear and uncluttered view" (Rawls 2001, 8) of the subject matter so as to deal appropriately with a few crucial questions. Rawls is rightly adamant that he does not need to apologize for the abstract and supposedly unworldly character of his philosophy (Rawls 1996, lxii).

It should be noted, however, that one need not apologize for the desire to make philosophical ideas concrete, either. As Alfred North Whitehead observed, "The true method of discovery is like the flight of an aeroplane. It starts from the ground of particular observation; it makes a flight in the thin air of imaginative generalization [think of the original position];

and it again lands for renewed observation rendered acute by rational interpretation" (1978, 5). To continue with this metaphor, the present book is meant to facilitate the landing of Rawls's theoretical craft, the most important in political philosophy since at least the time of the Wright brothers.

To be precise, this book is intended to fill the gap between Rawls's own empyrean heights and the really practical public policy proposals of government planners, lobbyists, and legislators. From the perspective of the latter, what I do in this book will look very theoretical and philosophical, whereas from the perspective of political philosophers, what I do in this book may appear somewhat pedestrian. But there is nothing wrong with walking. Indeed, the whole point of theoretical flights in political philosophy is to facilitate better walking. As I see things, both words in the title of the book are crucial: applied philosophy.

No doubt one of the reasons why Rawls did not do more in the area of applied philosophy was his fear that philosophers who achieve celebrity status in popular culture see their best arguments misunderstood and hence the philosophical enterprise itself diluted. But Rawls himself stresses the importance of nonideal theory as well as ideal theory, at least as long as the latter guides the former. In any event, Samuel Freeman astutely alerts us to the fact that the great political philosophers of the modern period have typically had their greatest practical influence in the centuries after they wrote: Locke lived in the seventeenth century but greatly influenced the revolutions of the eighteenth; Smith lived in the eighteenth century, but his greatest influence was in the nineteenth and twentieth; Marx lived in the nineteenth century, but the communist revolutions in his name occurred in the twentieth. It is not unreasonable to hope that liberal democracies in the twenty-first century will be more Rawlsian than they were in the twentieth (see Freeman 2007b, 5, 458, 472; Pincus 2009). Further, the recent collapse of communism in eastern Europe and the recent financial crisis brought about by a relatively unconstrained version of capitalism provide apertures for Rawlsians to think anew about the praxic implications of justice as fairness.

The "in-between" status of the present book is not unique, in that excellent work has been done over the past several decades (most recently by Freeman, Thomas Pogge, and Percy Lehning) in exploring the implications of Rawls's thought for practical issues like the just distribution of income, fair tax practices, inherited wealth, universal health care, defensible relations between church and state, the elimination of "the curse of money" on politics, and so on. But, as I see things, there is still significant "in-between" work to be done in several important areas, six of which are explored here. The problems that I examine mostly involve religion, either problems in political liberalism that bear on religion or problems in religion that bear on political liberalism.

My hope is that the "in-between" status of this book will actually make it instructive for scholars who are primarily interested in the intrinsically interesting theoretical issues in Rawlsian political philosophy, in that critical assessment of theoretical positions requires, in part, a consideration of how they play out in practice. It is also my hope that the book will be instructive for those whose interests in politics are primarily practical, in that solutions to practical problems are often stalled owing to disagreements at the theoretical level. That is, because neither theory nor practice can be conveniently ignored in political philosophy, the "in-between" status of the present book can be seen as one of its virtues.

In chapter 1 I try to explain and defend the Rawlsian method of reflective equilibrium. In this regard I enter into dialogue primarily with the traditional theist Nicholas Wolterstorff and his defense both of natural rights and of the (startling) claim that Rawls is a natural rights theorist. I emphasize that reflective equilibrium involves a *process* of justification, rather than a strictly ahistorical, algorithmic appeal to the deliberations that occur in the original position. This chapter is preparatory for the rest of the book because it enables us to understand the very practical ramifications of finding a place for natural rights in the Rawlsian universe. It also enables us to understand the transition from considered judgments to unconsidered consequences that characterizes applied philosophy in general. In this chapter I also discuss the thorny issue of how to justify the belief that human beings deserve political respect without Wolterstorff's appeal (and Rawls's own appeal, albeit at a very early stage of his career) to the *imago Dei* hypothesis that human beings are made in the image of God.

The second chapter explicates Rawls's complex views regarding the morality of war. I show that his stance is, for the most part, that of a just war theorist in the mold of Michael Walzer. Unfortunately, however, Rawls is also like Walzer in moving away from just war theory toward the realpolitik view of war in conditions of supreme emergency. I argue that Rawls's best contributions to political philosophy would be enhanced if he moved in the opposite direction, away from just war theory and toward pacifism. That is, I think that Rawls is sometimes mistaken about what he has discovered both in political philosophy proper and in terms of the practical ramifications of his discoveries. The long history of the religious tension between just war theory and pacifism is brought to bear in this chapter. I challenge Rawls's belief that principled opposition to war is more probably the result of religious conviction than of philosophical argument.

In chapter 3 I confront the difficult issue of how to deal with those nonrational yet sentient beings who have historically been left out of the social contract tradition: both mentally deficient human beings and non-human animals with central nervous systems. Here my interlocutor is Martha Nussbaum, whose capabilities approach supplements, rather than contradicts, Rawlsian social contract theory, on my interpretation. Further, I argue that the compatibility between the capabilities approach and social contract theory can be strengthened in terms of a revised original position that is more friendly toward the marginal cases of humanity and nonhuman animals than Rawls's own version of the original position. Here I confront the traces of the *imago Dei* hypothesis even in Rawls's later writings, specifically the anthropocentric character of that hypothesis, despite its ostensive theocentrism.

Chapter 4 is not as obviously concerned with religion as the other chapters, although even here I think it is fair to say that (a) defenders of legacy are the remote inheritors of the divine right of aristocracy and noblesse oblige, and (b) defenders of affirmative action often equate the quasi-religious and understandable battle against racism—e.g., the abolitionists were basically divine command theorists and Martin Luther King was a natural law theorist—with the questionable practices involved in affirmative action. In this chapter I try to supplement Robert Taylor's important treatment of this subject.

The fifth chapter deals with a crucial theoretical issue involved in the Rawlsian effort to understand how religious belief is compatible with responsible citizenship in a politically liberal society. Because many or most citizens in contemporary democracies are religious believers of some sort, the practical import of this understanding is hard to exaggerate. And the fact that many nonliberal societies are dominated by a certain kind of intolerant religious belief makes this issue especially important. Here I am especially concerned with Freeman's and Pogge's interpretations of issues related to religion and politics.

All of the chapters in the book can be seen as extended addenda to my previous book on Rawls, *Rawls and Religion: The Case for Political*

Liberalism, although the present book is intended to stand on its own and requires no familiarity with the previous work. The final chapter of the book is especially relevant in this respect. In this chapter I am concerned not so much with the implications of Rawls's political philosophy for issues related to religious beliefs but with Rawls's own religious beliefs themselves, or lack thereof. But even in this chapter my concerns will be Rawls*ian* rather than limited to Rawls's own religious beliefs or nonbeliefs.

In one sense it would have been appropriate to begin the book with the final chapter. However, because Rawls never intended that either of the texts involved—his very early undergraduate senior thesis while at Princeton and his very late testimony "On My Religion"—be made available to the public (they were published only posthumously, in 2009), I thought it best to conclude the book with this chapter. I want to show that the previous chapters can stand on their own without the (fascinating) evidence discussed in the last chapter.

My goal is not merely to trace the implications of Rawls's thought for these areas of philosophy but to illuminate these areas themselves. It is not self-evident how we are to think about natural rights, war, nonhuman animals, legacy and affirmative action, and religious belief in a democratic society. We very often need theory to understand and label, in some cases even to notice, the phenomena in question. That is, the project is rescued from any sort of Rawls scholasticism when it is noticed, again, that the title of the book refers to Rawls*ian* explorations rather than exegesis of Rawls's own texts. My goal is quite frankly to *use* Rawlsian insights so as to better understand several important practical problems in contemporary political life that matter to all of us, or to almost all of us.

I should also note the word "explorations" in the title of the book. As Whitehead once again puts the point, "the merest hint of dogmatic certainty as to finality of statement is an exhibition of folly" (1978, xiv). I try, nonetheless, to defend my views energetically, not because I believe that intensity of conviction translates into justificatory warrant but so as to play my part in the philosophical enterprise as well as I can. This enterprise is inherently dialectical, as I argue in chapter 1. My hope is that a spirited defense of certain theses will elicit equally spirited responses from scholars, in particular, and from those interested in approximating a just society, in general.

Finally, a word about my synoptic view of Rawls's career, a view that necessarily informs this book. Perhaps the key issue that has dominated

Rawls scholarship since the publication of *Political Liberalism* in 1993 is the relationship between the early and late Rawls. Clearly there is a great deal of both continuity and discontinuity between this work and *A Theory of Justice* (1971). The major discontinuity is that his view in the earlier work was often, but not always, articulated in terms of what he later called a comprehensive doctrine. His stance in later works was articulated in the more modest terms of political liberalism.

The overall thrust of my treatment of Rawls is based on the continuity in his writings. Here I follow Freeman rather closely. It should be noted that justice as fairness, the original position, the veil of ignorance, the priority of the right to the good, the two principles of justice, and so on, are all retained in the later Rawls under the umbrella term "political liberalism"; hence I will switch back and forth without qualification between "justice as fairness" and "political liberalism." Of course, I also indicate, when appropriate, where the views found in the early Rawls deviate from those in the later Rawls and where justice as fairness is not to be seen as equivalent to political liberalism, in that the latter designation is, to be precise, generic and includes justice as fairness as only one of its specific instances. An example of where the early Rawls differs from the later Rawls can be seen in his concept of stability: in the early Rawls stability is explicated primarily in terms of congruence (between the right and the good), whereas in the later Rawls stability is explicated in terms of overlapping consensus. For the most part, however, *Political Liberalism* and other later writings build on or clarify *A Theory of Justice*, in my view.

There are four notable discontinuities between the early and late Rawls: (1) In *A Theory of Justice* there is no clear distinction, as there is in *Political Liberalism*, between moral philosophy in general and political philosophy in particular; (2) thus there is no clear distinction in *A Theory of Justice*, as there is in *Political Liberalism*, between a moral, comprehensive view of justice and a political conception of justice; (3) the idea of stability as congruence in *A Theory of Justice* is especially problematic, in contrast to the concept of overlapping consensus in *Political Liberalism*; and (4) Rawls admits in *Political Liberalism* that he had underestimated, in *A Theory of Justice*, the difficulty of making his idea of a well-ordered society consistent.

But these discontinuities between the two works are still perfectly compatible with an overall thesis of continuity. In fact, in order to even understand the nature and extent of the problems listed in the previous paragraph, one must see them as arising from a point of view internal to justice as fairness as that concept is developed in both the 1971 book and the 1993 book. Rawls himself speaks of a "unity" of both "spirit and content" in *A Theory of Justice* and *Political Liberalism*. Once the problems in the previous paragraph are addressed, the structure and content of the two books are, as Rawls notes, "the same." The ambiguities in *A Theory of Justice* are largely cleared up by presenting from the outset the idea of justice as fairness as a political, rather than as a comprehensive moral, conception (Rawls 1996, xvi–xix).

It is crucial for my aims in this book to emphasize that the major contributions of Rawls's later works are largely a result of Rawls's own explorations in religion and applied philosophy. It is my hope both to better understand and to expand on these contributions.

1

RAWLS, NATURAL RIGHTS, AND THE PROCESS OF REFLECTIVE EQUILIBRIUM

Nicholas Wolterstorff's *Justice: Rights and Wrongs* (2008) was hailed, on its dust jacket, by one notable critic as the most important work on the subject since Rawls's *Theory of Justice* in 1971. Quite a compliment! Wolterstorff's extremely interesting comments on Rawls raise important questions for how we should interpret Rawls's work. Specifically, Wolterstorff provides a most useful frame for considering Rawls's overall method of reflective equilibrium. He presses Rawls's defenders to account for their belief that human beings are free and equal, a belief that is an integral part of any effort to achieve reflective equilibrium in liberal democratic political theory. Wolterstorff's insistence in this regard (and his own traditional religious account of this belief) helps us develop a richer understanding of the method of reflective equilibrium. Granted, Wolterstorff is not criticizing the idea of reflective equilibrium per se; rather, he asserts that there is an unacknowledged reliance on natural rights in Rawls. But as a result of his criticisms, we acquire a much better understanding of the method of reflective equilibrium that will be at work in this book.

WOLTERSTORFF'S VIEW

Wolterstorff makes the startling but understandable claim that Rawls's theory of justice is an inherent natural rights theory (hereafter I will drop "inherent" and refer simply to natural rights theory), but that Rawls "does nothing at all to develop an account of such rights. He simply assumes their existence" (Wolterstorff 2008, 15). This is why Wolterstorff largely ignores Rawls; Wolterstorff is concerned with developing an account of natural rights. As he puts it, "my interlocutors will be those who do not just appeal to such rights but have something to say about them" (15). Because Wolterstorff's claim will shock many readers, we should ask why he claims that Rawls's early theory of justice is a natural rights theory. Wolterstorff's response to this question rests squarely on the work of two scholars, Michael Zuckert and Ronald Dworkin.

Zuckert's thesis is that, whereas Locke understood rights, and therefore justice, to derive from "property" (he used the term to include life and liberty), Rawls understood rights, and therefore justice, to derive from fairness. There is no idiosyncratic use of "rights" at work here; the term is used in a familiar way to refer to legitimate claims.

It seems that what Wolterstorff likes most about Zuckert's interpretation concerns Rawls's view of the inviolability of the human person. Whereas for Locke justice derives from the inviolability of the human person (i.e., from rights), which in turn is derived from property, Rawls takes almost the reverse stance: justice derives from fairness, and inviolability (i.e., rights) derives from justice. As Zuckert sees things, this stance jars our intuitive or commonsense notion of justice, in that we normally tend to think that justice follows from, and does not ground or serve as the source of, rights. In other words, the Rawlsian account of inviolability is in a state of disequilibrium with our intuitive or commonsense notion of justice.

Zuckert and Wolterstorff are in agreement with Rawls, and against utilitarian thinkers, in thinking that human beings are inviolable. For example, all three thinkers agree that the utilitarian critique of slavery is problematic because it condemns slavery only contingently. Under certain conditions a utilitarian might have to permit, or even encourage, slavery, as is well known. By contrast, Zuckert and Wolterstorff agree with Rawls that we should condemn slavery as a matter of principle.

The key criticism that Wolterstorff, with the aid of Zuckert, would like to make is that Rawls's defense of the inviolability of the person *should* be based on something like Locke's (and Wolterstorff's) concept of natural rights, a concept that relies on the biblical tradition of seeing a human person as an *imago Dei,* as being made in the image of God. Indeed, Zuckert suggests that Rawls's defense of inviolability *is in fact* "parasitic" on Locke's view. In this respect Zuckert and Wolterstorff are articulating the now familiar view, endorsed as well by David Ray Griffin and Jurgen Habermas (e.g., Griffin 2007, chapter 7; Habermas 2002), that various "postreligion" ethicists and political philosophers are living off the capital accumulated during the Christian ages; they conveniently receive a great deal of insurance without having to pay any premiums. (Think of the reductionistic biologist who sees human beings as so much protoplasmic stuff, as strictly accidental by-products of blind evolutionary history, but as nonetheless capable of belonging to Amnesty International. The issue here is not the theory of human evolution per se, which is perfectly compatible with many types of religious belief, but its reductionist materialist interpretation, which is very difficult to reconcile with any sort of religious belief, as we will see later in the book.) But Rawls muddies the water by speaking as if the inviolability of human persons is not prior to justice as fairness but derived from it.

Zuckert is not alleging foul play or subterfuge on Rawls's part. Rather, he thinks that Rawls is led into genuine confusion as a result of his belief that there no more could be justice outside of (democratic) practices than there could be strikeouts outside of the practice of baseball. An athlete could swing a stick in the air three times, but outside of the practice of baseball this would not be a strikeout. Likewise, outside of certain political practices there could be no rights and hence no inviolability of the human person, on Zuckert's interpretation of Rawls, adopted by Wolterstorff. On this interpretation, a Rawlsian would presumably have to admit that "Hugo would be perfectly in the right to gratuitously kill Samuel if they met on a desert island" (Zuckert 2002, 327). Rawls would be better served, Zuckert thinks, if he considered "more carefully the preconditions for his own edifice of fairness" (327; see also Seagrave 2009).

Several features of Dworkin's liberal critique of Rawls do not figure in Wolterstorff's account. It is Dworkin's treatment of Rawlsian reflective equilibrium that positively influences Wolterstorff, who has complained about the "inarticulate" nature of Rawls's epistemology, such that interpreters of Rawls have to engage in an inordinate amount of exegetical industry in order to figure out what Rawls means by reasonableness, rationality, and reflective equilibrium (see Wolterstorff and Audi 1997, 69, 75, 77–79, 98–99, 109, 111–12, 148). I will assume, however, that reasonableness can be understood as the willingness to abide by fair terms of agreement and that rationality can be understood as the ability to follow arguments and the like. Whereas it takes a reasonable person to be willing to enter the original position and to abide by the decisions made there, it takes a rational person to do the deliberating.

Dworkin, however, correctly makes it clear that it is a mistake to assume that there is a direct, one-way argument from the original position to Rawls's famous two principles of justice. This is a simplistic (because static) approach that is nonetheless the basis for the pedagogy through which many or most students come into contact with Rawls's thought. Dworkin rightly emphasizes that Rawls's more complex processual method consists in seeking reflective equilibrium "between our ordinary, unreflective moral beliefs and some theoretical structure that might unify and justify these ordinary beliefs" (Dworkin 1977, 155).

On the one hand, the method involves the effort to provide a structure of principles that supports (i.e., that unifies *and* justifies) our ordinary, unreflective moral beliefs. On the other hand, we should also be prepared to alter or even abandon immediate convictions in the face of powerful theory. "We can expect to proceed back and forth between our immediate judgments and the structure of explanatory principles in this way, tinkering first with one side and then the other, until we arrive at what Rawls calls . . . reflective equilibrium in which we are satisfied, or as much satisfied as we can reasonably expect" (Dworkin 1977, 156). Dworkin notices, as few critics do, that for Rawls (and for Dworkin himself, if not for Wolterstorff) the conditions that are embodied in the description of the original position are not imposed from without but are those that we either do in fact accept or could be led to accept as a result of the process of philosophical reflection (158–59, 169; Rawls 1999c, 19, 514).

Dworkin, along with many commentators, sees reflective equilibrium as part of a coherence theory of morality. But unlike most commentators, he sees two sorts of coherence. One of these is "natural," wherein human beings have a moral faculty that enables them to discover eternal and static moral reality, as in the intuition that slavery just *is* wrong. This faculty is analogous to the physical observations in science that are the clues to the existence and nature of physical laws.

The second of these coherence models is "constructive," in which the practitioner of the type of moral philosophy found in the model does not assume that principles of justice have a fixed, objective existence, as in the natural model. For example, the intuition that slavery is wrong is not a clue regarding the existence of an independent, eternal principle but a stipulated feature of the general theory to be constructed.

Most commentators do not see the natural model as a type of coherence theory. Rawls would seem to agree with these commentators. Dworkin's classification of the natural model as a type of coherence theory seems to be the result of the analogy he draws with scientific observation. For example, if an astronomer has clear observational data that do not cohere with any existing theory, the astronomer understandably thinks that observational powers have temporarily outstripped explanatory powers and that the task is to try to have the latter catch up with the former so that coherence is eventually reached.

By way of partial contrast, when "observations" are made by a moral faculty, the situation is a bit more complicated, in that it is not automatically assumed that theory has to "catch up." This is because in the constructive model the "observations" regarding justice or injustice are more likely to be contested than in the natural model. There is something gained in the constructive model, however. Coherence is eventually reached owing to the responsibility and persistence of the moral agents who take initial intuitions regarding justice or injustice seriously along with the rational desire to be consistent. The point is not that scientific inquirers are not responsible or persistent. Rather, the idea is that, although these traits may facilitate coherence between observation and theory in science, they are not absolutely essential, as they are in the constructive model. That is, in the constructive model, moral philosophers themselves must *take responsibility for* the processual drive for coherence.

As before, Rawls's constructivist notion of reflective equilibrium is a two-way process that goes back and forth between adjustments to conviction and adjustments to theory until the most adequate fit is achieved. (On the natural model this might look like "cooking" the evidence.) Once again, reflective equilibrium is a *process* notion rather than an algorithm that gives us the right answer once and for all. Although such an algorithm might not be found in the natural model either, it seems fair to claim that scientists at least hope to approximate such algorithmic thinking.

If one's tentative theory of justice does not fit some particular intuition, this should serve as a warning that we should consider whether we really want to hold on to the intuition. Or perhaps it leads us to question the theory. The key point here is that the two-way process of reflective equilibrium is at odds with the natural model, which Dworkin thinks aims at the "timeless features of some independent moral reality" (1977, 166). It should be noted that, although Wolterstorff relies on Dworkin in his criticism of Rawls, Wolterstorff's own view of natural rights as ultimately resting on a theistic basis (on a traditional theistic basis at that, where God is seen as immutable) would seem to ally him with what Dworkin calls "the timeless features" of "the natural view." I will argue in due course that (despite the fact that I am a theist, albeit a process one) this gets Wolterstorff into trouble.

What is not in dispute among Dworkin, Wolterstorff, and Rawls is that a rights-oriented approach should be defended. For example, Wolterstorff and Rawls would agree with Dworkin that "there is a difference between the idea that you have a duty not to lie to me because I have a right not to be lied to, and the idea that I have a right that you not lie to me because you have a duty not to tell lies. . . . A theory that takes rights as fundamental is a theory of a different character from one that takes duties as fundamental" (1977, 171). The questions before us are how we should account for rights, and how rights fit into the processual method of reflective equilibrium.

Although Dworkin does not give a great deal of evidence of agreeing with the conservative elements in Zuckert's and Wolterstorff's views of justice, he does think, along with them, that Rawls's view is ultimately a natural rights position: "It must be a theory that is based on the concept . . . of rights that are *natural,* in the sense that they are not the product of any legislation, or convention, or hypothetical contract. I have avoided that phrase because it has, for many people, disqualifying metaphysical associations. They think that natural rights are supposed to be spectral attributes worn by primitive men like amulets, which they carry into civilization to ward off tyranny" (1977, 176). Dworkin tries to reassure his readers that Rawls's natural rights are not, as perhaps they are in Wolterstorff, parts of a "metaphysically ambitious" project (177).

Rather, they are connected to the practical political goal of protecting citizens. Nonetheless Dworkin admits, to Wolterstorff's delight, that natural rights are *assumed* by Rawls without argument in that they are "not simply the product of deliberate legislation or explicit social custom, but are independent grounds for judging legislation and custom" (177). Simply put, Rawls's social contract assumes natural rights even if Rawls himself prefers to think of his view as "ideal-based" rather than "right-based," and even if at times he tries to distance himself from any association with natural law (see Rawls 1999a, 400; 1996, 406).

Wolterstorff goes along with Zuckert and Dworkin in admitting that Rawls's presentation of his theory does not *appear* to be a natural rights theory. The argument that it is in fact a natural rights theory is strictly deductive, given other things that Rawls has to say. For example, it is basic to Rawls's theory that there be equal respect for all citizens, or at least for all reasonable/rational agents who *deliberate* in the original position. (More precisely, if the agents who deliberate in the original position are rational but not reasonable, this is because the information constraints they work under "stand for" reasonableness [Rawls 1999a, 317].) Wolterstorff unfortunately refers to agents who *bargain* in the original position, which confuses the Rawlsian original position with the Hobbesian state of nature (Wolterstorff 2008, 16; Rawls 1999c, 116n10, 120–21). The equal respect that is owed to those deliberating in the original position is due to . . . due to what? The Rawlsian response to this question would seem to involve a natural right to equality of concern and respect, "a right they possess not by virtue of birth or characteristic or merit or excellence but simply as human beings with a capacity to make plans and give justice" (Dworkin 1977, 182; see also Wolterstorff 2008, 16).

Wolterstorff cites two passages from Rawls himself to support the claim that Rawls's theory of justice in *A Theory of Justice* is built on natural rights. The first is in the main body of the text, where Rawls refers to equality as it applies to the respect that is owed to persons irrespective of their social position. This sort of equality is "fundamental," according to Rawls. He says that this type of equality "is defined by the first principle of justice and by such natural duties as that of mutual respect; it is owed to human beings as moral persons. The natural basis of equality explains its deeper significance" (1999c, 447; see Wolterstorff 2008, 16).

A second, more explicit, passage is found in a footnote. Its location outside the main body of the text Wolterstorff reads as a sign of Rawls's reluctance to parade the fact that his theory is built on natural rights, perhaps because of the aforementioned fear that he would be interpreted as advancing a metaphysically ambitious project.

No doubt it is this fear that scares away many potential readers of explicitly process philosophers like Alfred North Whitehead and Charles Hartshorne, both of whom were political liberals, it should be noted (see

Morris 1991; Dombrowski 1997c). This is unfortunate given their process contributions to political liberalism, most notably their defense of a version of theism wherein God is not an omnipotent king, the imitation of which gets in the way of democratic virtues, but is rather the ideal being-in-becoming who facilitates the liberal transition from force to persuasion (Whitehead 1961, chapter 5; Hartshorne 1984b; Dombrowski 2002b). This is no small accomplishment given that many or most people in the United States in particular, and in the world in general, are religious believers of some sort. Unfortunately, many of them have religious beliefs that contradict democratic virtues. Hence process theism is well positioned to try to persuade religious believers toward a better social world. Process or relational theism fits hand in glove with political liberalism even if it is but one among many reasonable comprehensive doctrines that are compatible with liberal citizenship, including many that are not religious. My hope in the present chapter is to add another process contribution to political theory by explicating the *dynamic* character of reflective equilibrium.

Now back to this second passage, where Rawls says that the fact that the capacity for moral personality is a sufficient condition for being entitled to equal justice "can be used to interpret the concept of natural rights."

> For one thing, it explains why it is appropriate to call by this name the rights that justice protects. These claims depend solely on certain natural attributes the presence of which can be ascertained by natural reason pursuing common sense methods of inquiry. The existence of these attributes and the claims based upon them is established independently from social conventions and legal norms. The propriety of the term "natural" is that it suggests the contrast between the rights identified by the theory of justice and the rights defined by law and custom. But more than this, the concept of natural rights includes the idea that these rights are assigned in the first instance to persons, and that they are given a special weight. Claims easily overridden for other values are not natural rights. Now the rights protected by the first principle have both of these features in view of the priority rules. Thus justice as fairness has the characteristic marks of a natural rights theory. Not only does it ground fundamental rights on natural attributes and distinguish their bases from social norms, but it assigns rights to

persons by principles of equal justice, these principles having a special force against which other values cannot normally prevail. Although specific rights are not absolute, the system of equal liberties
is absolute practically speaking under favorable conditions. (1999c,
442–43n30)

It is to Wolterstorff's credit that he highlights this footnote, for philosophers should not be startled to hear about the natural rights dimension
of Rawls's early theory. But my purpose in what follows is to interpret
this crucial statement in a way that differs somewhat from Dworkin's
interpretation and a great deal from Zuckert's and Wolterstorff's static
and religiously conservative interpretations.

Finding the best possible interpretation of this quotation is crucial if
we are to confront head-on Wolterstorff's claim that the deepest issue in
Rawlsian theory is one that is rarely discussed: the fact that the theory is
based on natural rights and that these rights must somehow be located
within the processual method of reflective equilibrium. From Wolterstorff's point of view, a theory of justice that is based on natural rights
should give us an account of these rights, and it *should* declare that a
society is just to the extent that it honors these rights. In this regard, it is
Wolterstorff's view, not Rawls's, that sees political philosophy in static
terms amenable to deductive explication. Rawls, Wolterstorff alleges,
does something different. He develops a theory of justice that appeals to
only one natural right: the right of rational agents (Wolterstorff should
say: reasonable/rational agents) to be treated with equal respect. On
Wolterstorff's view, Rawls wistfully hopes that if this natural right is hon-
ored, then all of the others will be secured (2008, 17).

CRITIQUE OF WOLTERSTORFF'S VIEW

One of the classic debates in moral theory concerns the question of starting points. Should we start with particular moral judgments or with general (or universal) moral principles? We can call those who defend the
former approach particularists and those who defend the latter general-
ists. The debate between the defenders of these two approaches is perhaps due to the fact that these thinkers are primarily interested in
different questions. The particularist is primarily interested in responding to the question, which actions are morally right (or wrong)? Whereas

the generalist is primarily interested in the question, what are the criteria of right (or wrong) actions?

Both of these views, it should be emphasized, are opposed to moral skepticism. But they combat moral skepticism in quite different ways. Despite the well-known and powerful Kantian arguments against particularism, some philosophers continue to insist that the best way to argue against moral skepticism is to start with particular moral judgments that are widely shared (e.g., that the mass killings at Auschwitz were unjust, that the treatment of Africans on the slave ships in the middle passage was immoral) and then try to work out the theoretical criteria for moral (or immoral) action later. Most of the major figures in the history of moral theory have made some contribution to this debate.

I understand Rawls's contribution to lie in his processual method of reflective equilibrium, which in effect asks the question, *why* does one have to choose between particular moral beliefs and general (or universal) moral principles when searching either for starting points in political philosophy (which is only one part of moral philosophy) or for the source of justificatory warrant? Rawls thinks it makes better sense to make use of *both* types of belief in the articulation and defense of moral theory. We sometimes begin a conversation in moral philosophy with a statement of a particular judgment; in other conversations we start with an affirmation of a moral principle, as in a statement of the golden rule. There is no good reason to restrict ourselves to only one of these starting points or sources of moral judgment (see DePaul 1988, 72). Or better, given that both particular moral judgments and general (or universal) moral principles are necessary conditions for, and perhaps jointly sufficient conditions for, moral discourse, the burden of proof should be on the person who wishes to crowd out one or the other of these features.

A partial response to Wolterstorff is available at this point. One of the reasons, but not the only one, why Rawls does not talk more about natural rights is that they collectively function only as a *part* of a theory of justice, rather than as its cornerstone, as in Wolterstorff. That is, Wolterstorff needs to manage his expectations regarding the place of natural rights within the Rawlsian processual method of reflective equilibrium. He should not expect natural rights to play as large a role in Rawls's thought as they play in Locke's thought. There are many ways to incorporate the strengths of both particularism and generalism, of course, and reflective equilibrium is only one of them. But by pointing out the hybrid character of the method we can trim Wolterstorff's expectation that if natural rights are in play they must take center stage. As in process thought in general, reflective equilibrium is thoroughly *relational* in character.

The mereological character of natural rights in Rawls's thought is signaled by the fact that he prefers to label his view "conception-based" or "ideal-based," rather than "rights-based," despite the obvious part that rights play. But his view is nonetheless "right-based," in the singular, so as to signify the Rawlsian commonplace that the right is prior to the good (Rawls 1999a, 400–401; Freeman 2007a, 18–19, 24).

As Freeman sees the issue, in Rawls's revival of "the natural rights theory of the social contract" there is a transition to a reflective equilibrium that involves "separate strands of argument," much like Peircian strands of cable that mutually reinforce one another and unlike the metaphor that a chain of argument is only as strong as its weakest link. That is, the cable metaphor comes closer to what reflective equilibrium is all about than the chain metaphor does—indeed, the chain metaphor has become so familiar that it is usually not even perceived as a metaphor (Freeman 2007b, x, 42).

By considering the many situations in which moral questions arise (i.e., by trying to incorporate the legitimate insights of moral particularists), we are inevitably led, whether explicitly or implicitly, to moral principle and to a region much wider than, but admittedly not at odds with, natural rights. As Michael DePaul puts the point, "most people have both general and particular initial beliefs" (1988, 79), including both general and particular beliefs about natural rights. But the key question is, how are we to bring these disparate beliefs into some sort of consistent whole? Particular beliefs, including particular beliefs about natural rights, can lead to disaster if they are not examined from some sort of reticulative perspective like that taken by the person who aspires to reflective equilibrium or the person who thinks systematically along the lines of Whitehead or Hartshorne. Robert Nozick's version of libertarianism, to cite one example, involves some extremely questionable judgments based on a runaway version of natural rights. Do we really want to privatize both the national park system and the public school system, as seems to be required by his version of libertarian theory?

Although there are clear differences between natural rights and natural duties, an important similarity between the two should not escape our notice. Natural duties are those that all reasonable beings already agree to and thus need not be adjudicated by a fair decision-making procedure.

We do not need a social contract to determine that cruelty is wrong. The natural duty not to be cruel holds between persons regardless of their institutional relationships, hence "the propriety of the adjective 'natural'" (Rawls 1999c, 99). No matter what comprehensive doctrine one believes in, if the doctrine is reasonable it includes the belief that we have a duty not to be cruel and a duty not to murder. This latter duty would thus apply even on a desert island, contra Zuckert. In this regard we should notice that Rawls incorporates the best from Hobbes and Locke regarding the concept of natural duties (Rawls 2007, 37, 43, 118–21, 144–46; see also Freeman 2007b, 418, 422).

Likewise, there is something antecedent about natural rights. These are the rights that are presupposed by the process of reflective equilibrium, as Wolterstorff rightly notes. But this need not be a problem, as Wolterstorff assumes. "The way in which it is rational for a person to resolve a conflict between beliefs will not be determined by which of those beliefs is general and which is particular, but by which belief seems most likely to be true to the person after thoroughly considering the matter" (DePaul 1988, 80). Once again, appeal to particular natural rights is only a part of the process of developing a defensible theory of justice. That the original position, or some other device used to develop a fair decision-making procedure, is needed indicates that the critic who alleges that reflective equilibrium leans more in the direction of generalism than particularism is on to something. But the method is hardly an attempt to run roughshod over particular moral beliefs. It is quite possible for theory as well as intuition to be overridden. The process of reflective equilibrium here looks similar to Whitehead's famous metaphor in *Process and Reality,* quoted in the preface. Theory is like an airplane that takes off from the ground (of particular intuitions) so as to develop an abstract account of the phenomena in question, making sure eventually to touch ground again (Whitehead 1978, 5).

The place of natural rights in Rawlsian political theory is further contextualized when a distinction is made between reflective equilibrium, as I have described it thus far in political liberalism, and the effort to find equilibrium between political principles and nonpolitical principles in philosophy of mind, science, and so on (see Daniels 1979). In both endeavors there is an understandable reluctance to give up on a seemingly well established belief (e.g., that cruelty is wrong) when challenged by an untested one. And in both there is the requirement of intellectual honesty, such that an inconsistent or poorly supported belief is relinquished in the face of a more powerful one that is internally consistent.

The starting points in the process of reflective equilibrium can be seen as shared notions latent in common sense (Rawls 1999a, 327), but this does not mean that they are self-evident. Both Rawls and Wolterstorff are understandably opposed to the idea of self-evident starting points (see Rawls 1999c, 18–19, 42–45). Or at least self-evident starting points, if such a thing exists, would have to be analyzed critically along with other proposed starting points (Rawls 1999a, 288–91). Wolterstorff even goes so far as to claim that the appeal to self-evident rights in the U.S. Declaration of Independence is "a piece of epistemological bluster" (2008, 319n). In Rawlsian language, to say that our starting points have some basis in our common democratic heritage is obviously not to say that they are metaphysically basic moral truths. In fact, they are clearly open to revision (Ebertz 1993, 196–97, 200, 212). (Nonetheless, some starting points—e.g., that cruelty is wrong—when revised put all of our other moral beliefs into a dangerous disequilibrium.) As Whitehead put a related point, the deadly foe of morality is not change but stagnation (1961, 269).

It is often noticed that behind the initial beliefs that get the process of reflective equilibrium started lies a Rawlsian view of the human person. At times Rawls distinguishes between *conceptions* of the human person and *ideals* of the human person (1999a, 321–22, 352). The former are connected, once again, to issues in philosophy of mind regarding, say, personal identity over time, whereas the latter are connected to issues in moral philosophy regarding how a human person ought to act and what a human person ought to be. It should be emphasized that, although there may well be useful connections between conceptions of and ideals of the human person, conceptions of the human person underdetermine moral theory. Even if Rawls himself seems to believe in a Kantian conception of the human person (as free, equal, reasonable, and rational), which pushes strongly in the direction of human rights, he is well aware that competing conceptions of the human person must be considered in a politically liberal society.

Granted, there are only a finite number of conceptions of the human person that see human persons as reasonable. And granted, each conception of the human person makes some moral theories more probable than others (Brink 1987, 81–86). But even if one grants these points, one is still able to defend the thesis that conceptions of the human person underdetermine moral theory. For example, to grant that a human person is made in the image of God still leaves unresolved many of the most important issues in political philosophy. Among Catholics, say, who believe in the *imago Dei* hypothesis, we find liberation thinkers who are heavily influenced by Marxist thought, Opus Dei members who consort with fascism, and political liberals, broadly construed. Luckily, this last group is the largest of the three.

The treatment thus far of the problem that the process of reflective equilibrium is meant to solve makes it possible both to better situate the place of natural rights in Rawls's view and to better understand the place of starting points within the process of reflective equilibrium.

But one of the difficulties that any interpreter of Rawls must confront is how to navigate among three different methods or types of justification in his thought: (1) the processual method of reflective equilibrium; (2) the original position, which can be understood as that part of reflective equilibrium wherein particular beliefs or intuitions regarding justice are put to the test of objective rationality; and (3) public reason, which is more restrictive than reflective equilibrium in general because it concerns only those values that can be affirmed by all reasonable beings regardless of the comprehensive doctrines they affirm. Regarding (3) it can be said that not all considered judgments meet the publicity criterion (e.g., those that concern religious beliefs). Like the original position, public reason can profitably be seen as part of the process of reflective equilibrium, the part that deals with concepts that constitute an overlapping consensus with other reasonable citizens on the subject of justice (Rawls 1996; Dombrowski 2001a). The original position is admittedly, in a way, deductive and nonprocessual, but reflective equilibrium as a whole is a process.

However these three methods or types of justification are related, it is requisite that we understand reflective equilibrium itself as including three moments: identifying initial beliefs or intuitions about justice, trying to account for these from some objective point of view, and trying to reach equilibrium when the previous two moments diverge. Equilibrium, it should be noted, is a goal or an ideal rather than an accomplished fact; thus we should be wary of having our starting points do too much work for us, as Thomas Scanlon emphasizes (2003, 139–41).

Scanlon is also helpful in distinguishing between descriptive and deliberative understandings of reflective equilibrium. Whereas the former

enables us to better understand the implications of what we already believe about justice, the latter enables us to better understand what we
ought to believe. Once again, the former provides some reason for a conservative understanding of reflective equilibrium, and the latter does the
same for a radical understanding of it, as when Norman Daniels has us
notice that a society that conformed to Rawls's three principles of justice
(the first principle—the equal liberty principle—plus the two parts of the
second principle, the equality of opportunity principle and the difference
principle) would be more egalitarian than any existing society, including
the social welfare states (Daniels 2003, 243; Rawls 2001, 135–40, 158–
62)! Although there is no compulsion to steer the method of reflective
equilibrium into the descriptive mode, it must be admitted that the
method does require that we account for those judgments concerning
which we are most confident, including judgments regarding natural
rights (Scanlon 2003, 142–44).

One of the most common mistakes that interpreters of Rawls make is
to assume that Rawlsian justification occurs only within the deliberation
in the original position. But Rawls is quite clear that "justification is a
matter of the mutual support of many considerations" (1999c, 507). That
is, reflective equilibrium is both thoroughly processual *and* thoroughly
relational in that all of the elements can be revised in light of the others.

If there are no good grounds for doubting our beliefs, it is reasonable
to grant them initial credibility and a fallible authority. It is not merely
that we believe them that counts, but that they are credible, as Wolterstorff would otherwise admit as a reformed epistemologist. The stance of
reformed epistemology involves an innocent-until-proved-guilty quality:
we should be free to believe whatever we wish until the belief is shown
to be inconsistent, contradicted by the facts, and so on. Rawls is rightly
most famous, however, for the deliberations that occur in the original
position, so it makes sense for Scanlon to say that if we had to choose
between the descriptive and the deliberative understandings of the processual method of reflective equilibrium, the latter deserves the nod. At
least in principle, our initial judgments can change significantly over the
course of time in that reflective equilibrium is not only a process but a
"Socratic" process. It is because this method is self-correcting that Scanlon says that it is "the best way of making up one's mind about moral
matters and about many other subjects. Indeed, it is the only defensible
method" (2003, 149).

This is a remarkable claim. But I do not think that Scanlon hyperbo-
lizes here, for the process of reflective equilibrium is exactly what is required if we are to avoid the twin evils of reifying either particular moral
judgments or general (or universal) moral principles. Reflective equilibrium is process ethics at its best (see also Henning 2005).

It must be admitted that at times Rawls gives the impression that
principles of justice are *given* to us by practical reason, but because it is
our practical reason that does the giving, I assume that there is no big
problem with this impression, in that human actions are shaped by self-
examination and criticism. And it is this criticism that prevents contractarianism from degenerating into conventionalism. Reflective equilibrium
is an ideal, it will be remembered, rather than an already accomplished
fact; the process of modifying ideas and rejecting recalcitrant ones is
ongoing. In a later chapter we will see that this asymptotic effort is complicated considerably in the later Rawls by the fact that one must also
bring into equilibrium the principles of justice operative in politics with
one's comprehensive doctrine. The complications are especially noteworthy if the comprehensive doctrine in question does not have an obvious place for human autonomy (Freeman 2007a, 6, 27, 38, 40, 240;
Rawls 1996, 385).

To say that the method of reflective equilibrium is processual is to say
that one always begins one's thinking about justice in the middle of
things. One "starts" with intuitive considerations, but one does not exactly ground them, as Wolterstorff hopes to do in spite of his reformed
epistemology. One "then" moves to the original position, but the rational
deliberations found there are framed by the reasonable, which includes
the *desire* to abide by fair terms of agreement, a desire that is implied in
the willingness to deliberate under the constraints imposed by the veil
of ignorance. As Burton Dreben emphasizes regarding the process of
reflective equilibrium (Dreben is almost alone among scholars in explicitly referring to reflective equilibrium as a *process*), the key phrases in
Rawls, which have hardly been noticed, are "working through" or "working out." Rawls spent an entire career working through the fund of implicitly shared ideas in liberal democracies. His working out of the
concept of justice as fairness gave him more than enough to do; he ended
up contributing more to political philosophy than any other twentieth-
century philosopher. Further, he ended up a more consistent critic of
foundationalism than Wolterstorff, despite the latter's reformed epistemology. Or again, Rawls himself speaks not so much of "analyzing" the

idea of a just society as of "unfolding" it, as Freeman rightly emphasizes (Freeman 2007b, 337–38; Rawls 1996, 27).

Because one begins in the middle of things, the primary tasks in political philosophy consist not so much in refuting defenders of fascism like Heidegger or various defenders of Marxism (although Dreben does not mention that Rawls carefully examines Marx as a political philosopher [Rawls 2007, 319–72; 2001, 176–79]). Rather, one tries to explicate both the benefits of living in a liberal democracy and the conceptual details of what such a society ought to look like. "A basic task of political philosophy is to work out the best terms of what would be fair" (Dreben 2003, 336). This involves the search for a liberal constitutional democracy that is stable, but stable for the right reasons. This search, in turn, involves dialectic, as Rawls himself admits when he compares reflective equilibrium to Aristotle's dialectical procedure in the *Nicomachean Ethics*. In Aristotle there are starting points (*archai*), received opinions (*endoxa*), commonplaces (*topoi*), and, of course, habits ("ethics" is derived from the Greek word for habit, *ethos*) that enable us eventually to move dialectically *to* principle. But it is also possible to move *from* principle deductively. Both dialectic and deduction are required (see Hardie 1968, chapter 3; Rawls 1999c, 45).

Dreben confuses matters a bit when he compares the back-and-forth dialectical character of the process of reflective equilibrium with circular reasoning, which does not bother him. But because circular reasoning *does* bother most philosophers, it is better to stick with the claim that reflective equilibrium involves the give-and-take movement of dialectic at its best, wherein conceptual snags are untangled and inconsistencies exposed (Dreben 2003, 338). By contrast, Dreben is insightful when he says, "You cannot do substantial political or moral philosophy in any Cartesian-framed manner" (343), which is precisely (and ironically, given his reformed epistemology) what Wolterstorff tries to do when he tries to ground natural rights in the *imago Dei* hypothesis and then judge society's practice against the standard provided by such rights.

I would like to emphasize that Wolterstorff is to be commended for defending theistic philosophy with a capital "P." But I am not convinced that (1) theism has to be defended in the traditional, static terms Wolterstorff uses (see Dombrowski 2004a, 2005, 2006c), or that (2) philosophy with a capital "P" is appropriate in political thought, where the goal is to articulate fair terms of agreement among reasonable people with different, sometimes uncompromisingly different, comprehensive doctrines, including both religious and nonreligious ones (Rawls 1996). That is, Rawlsian political philosophy is no less important or difficult because it is done with a lowercase "p" (Dreben 2003, 346). As Hartshorne puts a related point, a liberal is one who knows that he or she is not God (1984a, 9).

To those who fear that the process of reflective equilibrium is relativistic, I would respond that although coherence is a necessary condition for justification in political philosophy, it is not sufficient. Common presuppositions in liberal democracies (e.g., that slavery and cruelty are wrong) and considered moral judgments in liberal democracies (e.g., that deviations from equality require justification) provide stable points that enable us to stave off the horrors of relativism. Roger Ebertz even goes so far as to refer to these stable points as "modest foundations" (1993, 206–7), such that the process of reflective equilibrium can profitably be seen not so much as opposition to foundationalism per se as to strong foundationalism. We should both allow the defender of slavery to state the case for slavery *and* insist that the extremely heavy burden of proof is on him, not his opponent. As Abraham Lincoln observed, "If slavery is not wrong, nothing is wrong" (quoted in Rawls 2001, 29; see also Mandle 2009, 40–41, 170–78).

Further, the method under consideration here is not equilibrium at any cost, which would indeed be relativistic. Rather, it is a method that involves a reflective, dialectically responsible process. Theories of justice should be viewed historically (i.e., processually) as involving concepts that are gradually purified in the fire of reasonable/rational criticism, with the best available concepts (considered judgments) providing preliminary standards for further dialectical criticism.

The provisional fixed points mentioned above (e.g., Lincoln's claim that if slavery is not wrong, nothing is wrong, which Rawls cites many times [see Lehning 2009, 34]) are sufficient to hold the wolf of relativism at bay. This is consistent with the claim that the content of public reason is not fixed, particularly if it is an expression of an especially dynamic society. Think, say, of how attitudes toward class, race, and gender have changed in liberal democracies over the past several decades. But even in the swift stream of contemporary history, the goal should remain to reach equilibrium between our real beliefs and what would be chosen in the original position behind a veil of ignorance. Overlapping consensus among reasonable beings is at least partially in place already, so this goal is not utopian in the pejorative sense of the term. Society's political conception should be publicly, though never finally, justified, as Rawls himself urges (1996, 388–89; see also Lehning 2009, 115, 122–25).

Or, more precisely, the realistic goal is that reasonable people would come to agree on a family of politically liberal views, of which justice as fairness is but one representative, albeit the most egalitarian member of the family. The Rawlsian hope for justice as fairness, in particular, is that other politically liberal views would cluster around it for comparison and contrast. It can be seen as a carefully defended "center of the focal class," as Lehning puts it, in the process of political justification (2009, 136, 144; see also Daniels 1996).

It is to be hoped that the processual character of the method of reflective equilibrium will become better known to both political philosophers in general and process thinkers (in the broadest sense of this designation) who are political liberals in particular, such that these two groups could help to further "work out" the concept of justice, which is, as Rawls emphasizes (1999c, 3), the first virtue of social institutions, just as truth is the first virtue of systems of thought.

It *is* well known that from the time of his doctoral dissertation and his first publication, Rawls was very much interested in a procedure that would correct our considered moral beliefs against a set of moral principles, a procedure that came to be known as reflective equilibrium. I have argued in this chapter, however, for a feature of reflective equilibrium that is not well known: that such equilibrium is not really a permanent state but a process (see Rawls 1999a, chapter 1; Pogge 2007, 15, 165). This realization changes things significantly, I think. For example, the familiar charge that Rawls's method is ahistorical and hence irrelevant to the flux of historical events begins to look inaccurate in the extreme.

In this regard it is worthwhile to consider the way that Rawls's views in *A Theory of Justice* were later clarified in *Political Liberalism.* As a result of the aftermath of the wars of religion, some defended a liberal, Enlightenment, comprehensive doctrine in an effort to replace religious comprehensive doctrines. In turn, this *comprehensive* liberalism is replaced by Rawlsian *political* liberalism, which is meant to be congenial to both religious comprehensive doctrines and skeptical comprehensive doctrines. For this reason, Rawls's explicit flirtation with natural rights (and with their implicit religiosity) in *A Theory of Justice* ends at the level of public, political discourse in *Political Liberalism,* even if the affair can nonetheless continue in the nonpublic realm of associational freedom.

2

A RAWLSIAN VIEW OF WAR

The purpose of this chapter is to explicate Rawls's views on war as they are scattered across several of his writings. That they are so scattered perhaps accounts for the paucity of scholarly attention paid to Rawls's view of war, which has, for the most part, remained consistent over the decades.

Three general positions are possible regarding the morality of war: (1) the just war position, which tries to determine and apply criteria for a moral war; (2) pacifism, which argues either that (a) war is not or cannot be moral, so one ought not to participate in it, or (b) war, if morally permissible, is nonetheless morally inferior to nonviolent resistance as a means of responding to disputes; and (3) the position that holds that war and morality are mutually exclusive, so we should not be distracted by moral considerations when faced with war or the possibility of war. This last position has no common name but appears under several rubrics: realism, military necessity, *inter arma silent leges,* "all's fair in love and war," "war is hell," and so on.

OPPOSITION TO REALISM

Integral to the realist view of war are the ideas that (a) the state has full control over the population (including minorities), resources, and so on, within its recognized territory, and (b) the state has the right to go to war in the rational (not necessarily reasonable) pursuit of its interests (Morgenthau 1978). A phrase roughly equivalent to (b) is found in Clausewitz's famous claim that war is "politics by other means."

By way of contrast, in the politically liberal, democratic states that Rawls defends, it would be unjust for the state to wage war strictly in the rational pursuit of its interests, as in wars for the purposes of the expansion of territory or true religion, or for inherently aggressive reasons. In fact, the only convincing reasons in favor of the claim that a politically liberal, democratic state is fighting with *jus ad bellum,* or a just cause, are that the state is fighting in self-defense or that it is intervening in unjust societies to prevent grave human rights violations (Rawls 2000, 359–60; 1999b, 8). That is, early modern states were unjust in asserting the realist doctrine that the state has the right to go to war in the rational pursuit of its interest, just as they were unjust (along with premodern states) in asserting that the state has a right to full control over its population.

There is thus some overlap between Rawls's view of war and what he identifies as the traditional Christian doctrine that a state should go to war only in self-defense. In this regard they are united in opposition to realism. But there are also obvious differences between Rawls's view and the traditional Christian doctrine, especially concerning the belief that the state has a right to control the religious beliefs of its population (Dombrowski 2001a; see also March 2009).

Politically liberal, democratic states cannot initiate a just war: "they go to war only when they sincerely and reasonably believe that their safety and security are seriously endangered" (Rawls 1999b, 90), or when the safety and security of others are at stake. A war of self-defense has as its aim the protection and preservation of basic freedoms, such that a politically liberal, democratic state fighting with *jus ad bellum* cannot do so (especially if it uses state power to force its citizens to fight) to gain economic wealth or to acquire natural resources, much less to establish an empire. However, any society that is even approximately just has a right to self-defense—for example, even a decent state that respects differences of belief in various comprehensive religious or philosophical doctrines on the part of its citizens, but that is ruled by oligarchs and is not democratic (Rawls 2000, 359; 1999b, 41–42, 84, 90–92).

The six Rawlsian characteristics of a just war as waged by a politically liberal, democratic state are as follows: (1) The aim of such a war is a just and lasting peace among peoples, especially with the present enemy. (2) It is assumed that in such a war the opponent is not democratic in that politically liberal, democratic states do not wage war against each other. Rawls relies here (1999a, 566) on a fascinating two-part article by Michael Doyle (1983), which concludes that even though liberal states have become involved in numerous (and sometimes unjust) wars with nonliberal states, constitutionally secure liberal states have yet to engage in war with each other. A remarkable claim! (3) Such a war involves both *jus ad bellum* (loosely, the justice *of* war) or just cause (i.e., self-defense or humanitarian intervention), on the one hand, and *jus in bello* (loosely, justice *in* war), on the other hand. *Jus in bello* involves, at the very least, discrimination between soldiers and civilians: "the grounds on which they [soldiers] may be attacked directly are not that they are responsible for the war but that a democratic people cannot defend itself in any other way" (Rawls 1999a, 566). The implication here might seem to be that civilians cannot be killed, but we will see that Rawls's position on noncombatant immunity is complicated. (In addition to soldiers and civilians, there are also the opposing state's leaders, the ones who are responsible for the aggression.)

(4) A politically liberal, democratic state must respect the rights of soldiers (e.g., when they become prisoners of war) and civilians on the opposing side because of the very nature of a politically liberal, democratic state. If *it* does not take human rights seriously, who will? (5) By its actions in war, a politically liberal, democratic state foreshadows the kind of peace that is the aim of a just war: "the way a war is fought and the actions ending it endure in the historical memory of peoples and may set the stage for future war" (Rawls 1999a, 567). And (6) the means-end reasoning used in war (e.g., in military strategies) must be framed within, and be strictly limited by, the first five principles. This last principle is part of Rawls's general commitment to circumscribe utilitarian reasoning by deontological constraints (Rawls 1999a, 565–67; 1999b, 37, 94–97; see also Freeman 2007b, 427, 434, 437, 472–74).

CAPITULATION TO REALISM

Rawls's general opposition to the realist view of war, which is consistent with the traditional Christian doctrine of just war theory, is not the whole story, however. In fact, under the influence of Michael Walzer's now classic study *Just and Unjust Wars*, Rawls concedes in part the realist's case (Rawls 1999b, 95, 98; 1999a, 566, 568–69, 571; see also Walzer 2006, especially chapters 14 and 16). The scope of realist opposition to just war theory covers both the *jus ad bellum* and the *jus in bello* dimensions of just war theory. That is, the thoroughgoing realist thinks that war and morality are mutually exclusive with respect to both the start of the war and the conduct of the war itself. Although Rawls often gives the impression that he is a just war theorist through and through, he is actually a just war theorist only with respect to *jus ad bellum* issues. He thinks that if one is fighting for a just cause, then one can, albeit in rare cases, suspend or override justice in the conduct of the war. In this respect he is very much like Walzer, as he admits, but he is also unwittingly like General Sherman in the American Civil War, whose claim that "war is hell" referred not to just cause, which Sherman thought was essential, but to *jus in bello* constraints (Rawls 1999a, 572; 1999b, 103; see also Walzer 2006, 32–33).

To be fair to Rawls, it should be emphasized that under most circumstances in war he defends *jus in bello* constraints. For example, he thinks that the firebombing of Tokyo and other Japanese cities in the spring of 1945, and the atomic bombing of Hiroshima and Nagasaki, all of which were primarily attacks on civilian populations, were "very grave wrongs" (1999b, 95, 102–3; 1999a, 568). However, Rawls's opposition to these civilian deaths is not part of a consistent, deontological condemnation of the killing of civilians in war.

There are two sorts of exception to *jus in bello* constraints that Rawls would permit. First, in several places Rawls indicates that enemy soldiers, but not civilians, may be killed directly in war (1999b, 96; 1999a, 566–67), leaving open the possibility that civilians may be killed indirectly. Although some scholars will find surprising Rawls's implicit use of the principle of double effect in these texts, it is very much consistent with Walzer's explicit use of it (Walzer 2006, 151–59, 257, 277, 280, 283, 317, 321; also Rawls 2007, 442). It should be remembered that Rawls himself says that his view of war does not differ in any significant respect from Walzer's, an admission that leads one to conclude that he is open to Walzer's use of the principle of double effect and the concept of utilitarianism of extremity (Rawls 1999b, 95). The sort of example that Walzer, at least, has in mind is found in the Allied raid on Vermork, Norway, in World War II, where civilians were knowingly killed in the effort to take out a heavy water plant the Nazis were constructing (Walzer 2006, 157–59).

At times Rawls suggests (mistakenly, I think) that attention should be paid to *jus in bello* constraints not because of the very nature of just war theory, dating back to the Middle Ages, wherein knowingly killing civilians is seen as inherently unjust. Rather, he thinks that attention should be paid to *jus in bello* constraints because of the devastation brought about by World War II (see Rawls 1999a, 554; 1999b, 26–27, 79, 102).

By apparently permitting the indirect killing of civilians in war, Rawls has left himself vulnerable to all of the traditional objections to the principle of double effect as it was used in theological casuistry. To ask just one question about this principle, what is the moral significance of saying that the killing of civilians in the Vermork raid was "indirect" when the bombers knew before the attack that these civilians would be killed if the plant were bombed? It is one thing to say that no moral wrong is done when civilians are killed in war as part of a genuine accident (as would have been the case if civilians had unexpectedly appeared at the heavy water plant at Vermork just at the time when the bombers attacked), and quite another to say that no moral wrong is done when civilians are knowingly killed (as was the case in reality, when the bombing plans were drawn up in full cognizance that the plant was in the middle of a civilian neighborhood). In the latter case it seems that the nonaccidental killing of the civilians was either morally permissible or not, such that the distinction between direct and indirect killing seems to have little or nothing to do with the key moral question. And the key moral question is whether one can ever knowingly kill civilians.

My own view is that such killing is unjust on straightforward deontological grounds. I may be wrong in my judgment, but the crucial points are that (a) Rawls has implicitly introduced, without argumentation, a very controversial use of the principle of double effect; and (b) Rawls, like Walzer, has also introduced means-end reasoning here that should be controversial on the basis of Rawls's own deontological commitments. I assume that if the killing of civilians in the Vermork raid was not a moral wrong, it would have to be due to some sort of utilitarian or cost-benefit reasoning that is not constrained by the usual Rawlsian deontological commitments.

Second, and even more troubling, is that, assuming for the moment the relevance of the Rawlsian distinction between direct and indirect killing of civilians, Rawls even permits the direct killing of civilians in war in conditions of what he calls extreme crisis (what Walzer calls supreme emergency). In these conditions civilians are killed not as an indirect by-product of what might be a legitimate target in war (e.g., a heavy water plant that was designed for the purpose of constructing nuclear weapons), but are killed directly.

How can such civilian deaths be justified? Here Rawls follows Walzer quite closely. Rawls condemns the bombing of Japanese cities in the spring of 1945 at least in part because there were alternative methods of bringing the war to a conclusion. At this late period in the war it was clear that the Allies were winning and that their victory was only a matter of time. But Rawls asks, "Were there times during the war when Britain could properly have bombed Hamburg and Berlin? Yes, when Britain was alone and desperately facing Germany's superior might; moreover, this period would extend until Russia had clearly beat off the first German assault in the summer and fall of 1941, and would be able to fight Germany until the end. Here the cutoff point might be placed differently, say the summer of 1942, and certainly by Stalingrad. . . . The crucial matter is that under no circumstances could Germany be allowed to win the war" (Rawls 1999a, 568–69). The definite "yes" in this statement (from an article originally published in 1995) is moderated in Rawls's treatment of the same subject matter in *Law of Peoples* (published in 1999). In the latter work he does not answer the question with a "yes" but with the following: "Possibly, but only if it was sure that the bombing would have done some substantial good" (1999b, 98–99). In both works, however, Rawls is clear that at no point in the war did Japan portend "incalculable moral and political evil for civilized life everywhere" (99), as did Nazi Germany. Thus, at no point in the war would it have been legitimate to kill Japanese civilians directly. Presumably, Rawls intends to show that the degree of evil must be quite high in order to bring about a supreme emergency or an extreme crisis, in partial contrast to the normal emergencies and crises faced by politically liberal, democratic states in war.

One cannot help but wonder at this point about the status of Rawls's own deontological constraints (again, see Rawls 1999a, 567; 1999b, 96–

97) that are supposed to hold in check the means-end reasoning and calculation that are common in war. Here Walzer is much more forth-right (if not more convincing) than Rawls concerning the claim that in some cases (albeit extreme ones, where civilized life itself is at stake) it is morally permissible to intentionally target and kill civilians. Walzer calls his position either "the utilitarianism of extremity" or (oxymoronically) "moral realism" (2006, 231, 326). We should note that these two designa-tions are not equivalent, as Walzer implies. A utilitarianism of extremity implies a close relationship between morality and war in that utilitarian-ism is, after all, a theory of morality. But the crucial feature of the realist's view of war, on Walzer's own line of reasoning, is the mutual exclusivity of war and morality (2006, chapter 1, "Against Realism"). In either case, however, there are significant deviations from Walzer's and Rawls's own versions of just war theory. In Walzer's terms, justice is "overridden" or "exploded" (231, 282). He sums up his just war theory/realism by saying that "we move uneasily beyond the limits of justice for the sake of justice (and of peace)" (282).

Once again, Rawls himself tells us that his view of war does not differ in any significant respect from Walzer's (1999b, 95). It should not be assumed, however, that there is a one-way influence from Walzer to Rawls in that Walzer indicates a debt to Rawls's implied sliding scale (on Walzer's reading of Rawls): the greater the justice of the cause, the more rules that can be violated in the conduct of the war (Rawls 1999c, 332; Walzer 2006, 229). Because Rawls tells us explicitly that his view of war does not differ in any significant respect from Walzer's, it seems that we can legitimately conclude that his view, like Walzer's, is a utilitarianism of extremity or a moral realism. Under most conditions in war, his view is a deontological one consistent with the respect-for-humanity version of the categorical imperative: one should not knowingly kill civilians in war, for this would be to treat them as means only. But it also seems legitimate to conclude that under conditions of extreme crisis his deonto-logical commitments are, like Walzer's, overridden.

Freeman's way of understanding the issue at hand is to say that be-hind the veil of ignorance it would be rational to agree to a range of circumstances in which there would be exemptions from perfect duties, like the duty not to kill civilians in war, quite apart from utilitarian calcu-lations that might otherwise be assumed to be central in such decisions. That is, in a supreme emergency the natural duty of justice not to kill civilians in a war with a just cause can be suspended. Freeman's appeal

here to the original position is meant to ensure that the publicity requirement is met because some "machinery of coercion" is required even
under favorable conditions, and such a requirement can withstand any
pacifist (e.g., Quaker) challenge (Freeman 2007a, 89–90, 93–95, 237;
Rawls 1996, 393–94). In due course I will claim that pacifism might be
defensible on some grounds other than those of a particular religious
sect. Indeed, it can be seen as rooted in political liberalism itself.

Two comments are in order. First, as I see things, there is a bigger
leap than Freeman imagines between a public justification of coercion or
violence directed against an attacker, on the one hand, and the same
justification directed against civilians, on the other. It is not obvious to
me, as it is apparently to Freeman, that reasonable/rational beings behind a veil of ignorance would agree to the latter. And second, it is not
clear which original position Freeman has in mind. As I understand
things, there are three uses of the original position in Rawls. There is the
famous use of it in *A Theory of Justice,* which may very well involve the
justification of the coercive power of the state but does not involve the
justification of war, much less of war directed against civilians. The other
two uses are found in *Law of Peoples* (e.g., 1999b, 70): one regarding
representatives from liberal democratic peoples and one regarding representatives from decent, hierarchical peoples who respect general human
rights, but not the particular liberal rights found among democratic peoples. In the second original position there would be no need to justify
violence against civilians, because liberal, democratic peoples do not war
against each other. There would only be warrant for affirming principles
traditionally found in just war theory, which include immunity for civilians. And it remains unclear how the third use of the original position
could loosen just war criteria so that violence against civilians could be
justified. It seems that such justification comes only from *abandoning*
traditional criteria for *jus in bello.*

PACIFISM AND POLITICAL LIBERALISM

The thesis of this chapter is that Rawls, like Lavoisier, has made a great
discovery, even if he is mistaken about its precise character. (Lavoisier is
given credit for discovering oxygen in the eighteenth century, although
he mistakenly thought that he had discovered "dephlogisticated air.")
Rawls thinks he has discovered why politically liberal, democratic states

must uneasily move beyond just war theory to realism (and then slip back again to just war theory when the extreme crisis is over), whereas the logic of his most lasting contributions to political philosophy should lead him away from just war theory and toward pacifism, at least in the second sense of the term mentioned above. In this regard I will try to separate Rawls's theory from the details of his own life, which was intimately connected to just war theory, both in support of the Allied cause in World War II (as a philosopher and as a member of the military) and in opposition to the United States' participation in the Vietnam War (see Pogge 1999, 1–15). (These details are extremely interesting, however: his head was grazed with a bullet in the war, leaving a scar for the rest of his life; he actually saw the remains of Hiroshima after it was struck with an atomic bomb, and so on—see Freeman 2007b, 3.)

Both Stephen Macedo and Marilyn Friedman have emphasized the claim sometimes made by Rawls (e.g., 2001, 40, 90, 181; 1996, 64) that political power is coercive power that must sometimes be used to contain threats to justice, and this on the analogy of a physician trying to contain a disease in a patient (see Macedo 1995; Friedman 2000). But we should be reminded here both of the separate peace that politically liberal, democratic states have made with one another (Rawls 1999b, 16) and of the fact that if such states go to war it should not be in order to gain wealth, power, and so on (Rawls 2000, 360). Further, coercive power is especially problematic if the state uses it to enforce one comprehensive doctrine at the expense of others, whether within a state or outside its borders (Rawls 1996, 37).

The whole point of political liberalism is to find a political conception with which all reasonable persons can agree, which is quite different from finding a common comprehensive doctrine. People once killed each other over religion, but they need do so no more in politically liberal, democratic states. Indeed, political liberalism arose in response to the wars of religion in order to find a way for reasonable people, who nonetheless differ uncompromisingly in the comprehensive doctrines that they affirm, to live together in peace.

Granted, the domain of the political always involves at least the threat of coercive power. But this does not mean that a just state would be characterized by Hobbesian stability, which is nonliberal in that it is based primarily on fear and brute force. Rather, the just state is stable for the right reasons, which are themselves entirely pacific (Freeman 2007b, 246–47, 468).

Rawlsians who are not pacifists will perhaps alert us at this point to a distinction implied in the later Rawls between (a) a *well-ordered society,* where people endorse approximately the same principles of justice and abide by them in the expectation that others will also abide by them, with this expectation regularized by the threat of coercion; and (b) a *kingdom of ends,* where all individuals have perfectly good wills and who consequently participate in an ethical commonwealth that reconciles all disputes without the use of coercion. The latter is "utopian" in the pejorative sense of the term, it will be alleged.

However, consider passages from three different books by Rawls, from different stages in his career, in this respect. In his later book *Lectures on the History of Moral Philosophy* (2000, 361–63), Rawls partially disagrees with Hegel's belief that war results from the anarchistic character of relations among states. The politically liberal view that Rawls defends sees the cause of war as rooted in the internal nature of states and not primarily in the anarchistic character of their mutual relations (although international anarchy is, no doubt, part of the story). Relying on Montesquieu and Kant, Rawls emphasizes that politically liberal, democratic states are peaceful among themselves because they have no reason to attack each other: they insist on freedom of religion and liberty of conscience, their industry and commerce meet their social and economic needs, and so on. The familiar historical (and mostly unjust) reasons to go to war, as in the imposition of a comprehensive doctrine on unwilling subjects, do not apply among these states.

In another later book (1999b, 19, 29, 44–54), Rawls makes the same point regarding the refusal of politically liberal, democratic states to impose their religious and other beliefs on others. Such states "limit their basic interests as required by the reasonable" (29), with the reasonable being characterized by such agreements as would be reached in an extension of the original position to include fair terms of agreement not only at a national level but also at an international level so as to constitute "the law of peoples." Politically liberal, democratic states tend to produce "satisfied" (if not cheerful or happy) peoples in that citizens in such states (a) can believe as they see fit within the limits of reason as established in an original position behind a veil of ignorance, (b) have basic needs met, and so on. This "peace by satisfaction" stands in contrast to an enforced "peace by power," to use Rawlsian phrases that are borrowed from Raymond Aron (Rawls 1999b, 47; see also Aron 1966).

"The intoxicating pride of ruling" (Rawls 1999b, 47) is quite simply at odds with Rawlsian justice as fairness, as is the very notion of a confessional state where everyone is forced to adhere to one comprehensive religious or philosophical doctrine (as in communism). If people mutually respect one another, they are easily persuaded of the concept of political equality among peoples. Rawls laments the fact that politically liberal, democratic states are still marked by considerable injustice, oligarchic tendencies, and monopolistic interests, factors that in large measure account for the fact that the separate peace among politically liberal, democratic states themselves often does not extend to relations between such states and nondemocratic states (with their "unsatisfied" peoples).

But Rawls hopes that in their relations with nondemocratic (or even outlaw) states, politically liberal, democratic states will be, in the long run, less likely to engage in war than nonliberal states. It should be noted that the liberal states that Rawls defends are not libertarian states, which allow excessive social and economic inequalities that are conducive to unsatisfied peoples and, as a result, to war. To be specific, a just and pacific society of satisfied people (see Rawls 1999b, 50) has at least five features (which supplement—or better, which further specify—the famous two principles of justice found in *A Theory of Justice*): (a) a certain fair equality of opportunity; (b) a decent distribution of income, so that citizens can take intelligent and effective advantage of their basic freedoms; (c) a societal employer of last resort, presumably so that all who want to work can do so; (d) basic health care for all citizens; and (e) public financing of elections so as to eliminate "the curse of money" (see also Rawls 1997, 772) from politics.

States that at least approximate these five ideals have never warred against one another; those that more closely approximate them (or that might actually reach them!) would necessarily extend the justice they exhibit internally to their external affairs with other states.

I would like to consider a third text from Rawls, this one from *A Theory of Justice*, where we can see quite clearly the tight connection that has always existed between Rawls's own theory of justice as fairness and pacifism, a connection that Rawls himself severs when he drifts toward realism in permitting (under certain circumstances) the intentional and direct killing of civilians in war. Rawls's better angels hover over him when he says the following:

> If pacifism is to be treated with respect and not merely tolerated, the explanation must be that it accords well with the principles of

justice. . . . *The political principles recognized by the community have
a certain affinity with the doctrine the pacifist professes.* There is a common abhorrence of war and the use of force, and a belief in the
equal status of men [sic] as moral persons. And given the tendency
of nations, particularly great powers, to engage in war unjustifiably
and to set in motion the apparatus of the state to suppress dissent,
the respect accorded to pacifism serves the purpose of alerting citizens to the wrongs that governments are prone to commit in their
name. . . . The warnings and protests that a pacifist is disposed to
express may have the result that on balance the principles of justice
are more rather than less secure. (1999c, 370–71 [emphasis added];
see also Mandle 2009, 107–8)

Thus, the affinity between the pacific character of justice as fairness and
pacifism itself has not gone unnoticed by Rawls. But by taking a detour
through realism, Rawls distracts his reader's attention away from Rawls's
own goal of a "realistic utopia," wherein the law of peoples, justified
through appeal to a second original position at an international level
(1999b, 32–34, 115), can bring about an international peace analogous to
the amelioration of internecine strife that has been the hallmark of politically liberal, democratic states.

A conceptual reversal can be detected here. In effect, the goals of
Christian and other religious pacifists are supported by political liberalism itself. Although the reasons for these various positions obviously
differ, the fact that they converge in their conclusion is worthy of notice
in that it might otherwise be erroneously assumed that pacifism is necessarily a sectarian view that relies, say, on imitation of the life of Jesus
when he is interpreted as a pacifist. The reversal consists in the realization that, whereas I think it is generally true that since the end of the
wars of religion in the early modern period liberalism has civilized religious believers, it is also true that countercultural pacifist religious believers have the very real potential to make political liberals more acutely
aware of one of their own core values. The core value I have in mind is
that differences among reasonable parties need not end in violence. Martin Luther King, Gandhi, Franz Jägerstätter, Lech Walesa, and others are
important figures to consider precisely because of the light they shed on
political liberalism. The long passage from Rawls quoted above demon-
strates that at one point in his career he agreed with what I have called
conceptual reversal.

TWO OBJECTIONS

Perhaps it will be stated that my position as developed thus far is insufficiently dialectical. Two important objections might be raised, each of which deserves careful response. First, it might be objected that on the basis of my proposal (that political liberals should move away from just war theory and toward pacifism), only disaster will follow; for example, as Rawls implies, pacifism did not provide a viable option when dealing with Germany in the 1930s and 1940s. That is, it will be objected that war and perhaps civilian casualties are the only viable options when dealing with this type of state, such that Rawls's transition from just war theory to realism is perfectly understandable.

A second, related objection might be made that original positions at an international level presuppose that those in these original positions are reasonable and willing to cooperate with those who have comprehensive doctrines different from their own. (I thank Alan Tomhave for this objection.) In the case of the second original position, this assumption seems safe, a bit less so in the case of the third original position. But there are some states that are not even candidates for the third original position. What is the pacifist going to say to representatives of an outlaw state that harbors terrorists who are bent on killing civilians? Or again, how could a pacifist (or even a just war theorist) respond to a new kind of war where the enemy is not necessarily another state but a network of unreasonable terrorists who are capable of hiding within the civilian population?

I will deal primarily with the first objection. In my response to this objection I hope to shed some light on what could be said in reply to the second. One should call into question the just war theorist/realist view of nonviolent resistance as admirable in some romantic sense but as flawed in practice when confronted with the likes of Hitler or states that harbor terrorists. I would like to stipulate a distinction between *anesthesia* (see Whitehead 1961, 256, 259, 275, 285–86), by which I mean inactivity in the face of evil, and *nonviolent resistance* or pacifism, by which I mean the sort of *activity* in the face of evil practiced by Gandhi and Martin Luther King.

Consider A. J. P. Taylor's tour de force *The Origins of the Second World War* (Taylor 1962; Robertson 1971). Painted with a rather wide brush, Taylor's thesis can be put as follows (or at least this is how Taylor is usually interpreted): World War I was called the "war to end all wars." In the wake of that terrible conflict arose a whole generation of pacifists, and appeasers, and isolationists in Great Britain, France, and elsewhere. When Hitler came to power in Germany, little resistance was offered to him by the quasi-pacifist and quasi-isolationist governments that had the power to offer resistance. By the time resistance *was* offered, Hitler's power had snowballed to such an extent that he could not be stopped short of a second world war. Thus, Taylor is alleged to say, although the primary cause of the war may lie with Hitler and the Nazis, the secondary cause of the war was the failure to use force by those who could have used force. A stitch in time (e.g., stopping Hitler's remilitarization of the Rhine) could have saved nine (million or more lives). All of this can be seen more simply in the microstructure: if A (a big brute) attacks B (a ninety-eight-pound weakling), then C (a good, but strong, person) has an obligation to intervene if C sees what A is doing to B. If C does not forcefully intervene, then B (or anyone else) has a right to claim that C is as unjust, or almost so, as A. Rawls seems to agree with Taylor on these important matters.

I am arguing that the difference between anesthesia and nonviolent resistance to evil, as I have defined these terms, can be illustrated not only in the lives of Gandhi, Martin Luther King, and others but also in what most just war theorists and realists, including Rawls and Walzer, would regard as the most difficult case of all for the nonviolent resister: how to respond to Hitler. The nonviolent tactics of Gandhi and King, it is often alleged, worked precisely because they were dealing with the British and the Americans, respectively, and not with Hitler or with states that harbor terrorists. My aim in discussing Hitler is to call into question the claims that nonviolent resistance to evil is weak and flabby, as is anesthesia; that nonviolent resistance to evil produces a deficiency of social awareness; and that the nonviolent resister fails to face the tragedy of human existence.

Surprisingly, a small step can be made in defense of my view by a more careful consideration of Taylor himself, whose position is not as unambiguous as I indicated above. Toward the end of his highly influential book he makes the following crucial points regarding World War II: "Men will long debate whether this renewed war could have been averted by greater firmness or by greater conciliation; and no answer will be found to these hypothetical speculations. Maybe either would have succeeded, if consistently followed; the mixture of the two, practiced by the British government, was the most likely to fail" (Taylor 1962, 278).

"Greater firmness" would have been Winston Churchill's approach. But Neville Chamberlain's appeasement approach, the one that failed, does not exhaust the possibilities. That is, appeasement is not the same as nonviolent resistance. Appeasement is the "mixture" Taylor alludes to, which in effect drew lines in the sand at Versailles and threatened Germany with retribution if it crossed those lines. And when Hitler crossed one line and nothing happened, and then another. . . . But if nonviolent resistance is interpreted not only as an opposition to violence as a means of settling disputes but also as an opposition to threats of violence, a nonviolent resister never would have been party to the Treaty of Versailles in the first place. As Taylor suggests, nonviolent resistance or "greater conciliation" might have succeeded as well as "greater firmness." Although Rawls and Walzer would presumably agree with Churchill's "greater firmness" approach, it should be noted that the lengthy quotation from Rawls's *A Theory of Justice* at the end of the previous section is compatible with Taylor's point regarding the possible efficacy of "greater conciliation." That is, rapprochement with Rawls can be reached when it is realized that (a) for Rawls, the supreme emergency exemption should almost never be invoked; and (b) Rawls's defense of liberal democratic theory itself bears striking resemblances to the pacifist position.

Of course we will never know if nonviolent resistance would have succeeded against Hitler on a large scale, but the point is that the just war theorist or realist cannot legitimately claim to know that it would not have succeeded, as Taylor acknowledges. It seems unfair to blame the nonviolent resister for the consequences of the Treaty of Versailles. Violence (and threats of violence) breeds violence. An absence of these sorts of threats and a conciliatory economic policy (as advocated by John Maynard Keynes [Keynes 1920]) might have taken away the breeding ground for Hitler and the Nazis. But even if Hitler would still have come to power, it might have been possible to nip him in the bud in the early 1930s or at any other time through Gandhi-like nonviolent resistance from massive numbers of (religious or other) citizens. The various (religious) groups in Germany, however, failed to promote nonviolent resistance, not because they were skeptical of its efficacy but rather because they were not necessarily opposed to Hitler. In fact, as is well known, some religious leaders (who were just war theorists, no doubt) greeted Hitler with open arms and even made agreements with him. In short, it has not been shown that nonviolent resistance could not have worked either against or in Germany.

As I see things, the Rawlsian view should be that reliance on force, or at least reliance on force alone, is empirically inadequate and morally objectionable in the effort to approximate either a just state or a just international order. Or again, a widespread and effective sense of justice either in a society or among societies sustains justice far better than "a clever set of threats and inducements" (see Pogge 2007, 193–94).

It must be admitted that the phrase "or at least reliance on force alone" in the previous paragraph is crucial and deserves further attention, especially if some sort of rapprochement is to be reached with those who are not pacifists. The term "pacifism" can mean either (a) a strict opposition to violence as a means of settling disputes, or (b) a commitment to the belief that violent resistance to evil is morally inferior to nonviolent resistance to evil as a means of settling disputes. The latter meaning is obviously less demanding than the former and suggests that there is a continuum between certain types of pacifism and certain types of just war theory. That is, those just war theorists (cf. Walzer 2004, 86–89) who emphasize that a just war is one that is fought as a last resort are on a continuum with, or perhaps overlap, those pacifists who hold (b). In both views nonviolent resistance should be seriously tried before violence is used. For example, in domestic affairs the approximation of a just society tends to reduce the very need for conflict resolution with violent criminals, encourages the use of sedative darts or Tasers before the use of lethal force, involves the effort to bring about reconciliation with criminals once they are sequestered from society, and so on.

This sort of rapprochement between pacifism and just war theory is illuminated by Rawls's views on civil disobedience and conscientious refusal (1999c, sections 53–59). Under nonideal conditions, civil disobedience takes precedence over violence simply because its features are more consistent with ideal theory, specifically concerning the requirement that fellow citizens be addressed in a public manner and with respect. Of course the just war theorist will point out that this does not rule out violent resistance if nonviolent resistance fails, but it does highlight the fact that nonviolent resistance is morally preferable to violent resistance. Something parallel to this could be said at the international level. In order to model liberal principles in international relations, we should start with diplomacy and an array of other nonviolent measures before violent ones are used.

SOME EXAMPLES

No doubt my argument thus far seems a bit abstract, in the pejorative sense of the term. To say that one cannot prove that nonviolent resistance would have failed in response to Hitler and the Nazis does not exactly show that there is any likelihood that it would have succeeded. In this penultimate section of the chapter, however, I would like to argue that in the few cases where nonviolent resistance to Hitler and the Nazis was attempted, it achieved enough success that it is at least plausible, indeed it is quite likely, that a more extensive use of nonviolent resistance could have radically altered history in the disastrous period between 1933 and 1945. My goal here is, obviously, not to do historical research but rather to use the historical research of others, as summarized by Nathan Stoltz-fus, in the effort to support the philosophical case for nonviolent resistance, in partial contrast to Rawls (see Stoltzfus 1992; Kershaw 1987, 1999; Stern 1975; Zahn 1989; Dombrowski 1991). Let us consider three cases in particular.

(1) There is apparently only one recorded instance where Germans of the Third Reich protested on behalf of fellow citizens who were Jews. Until early 1943 the Nazi regime had exempted Jews married to "Aryans" from the "final solution." But on February 27, 1943, there was a mass arrest of the last Jews in Berlin, the *Judaschlusaktion* (the final roundup of the Jews). Ten thousand were arrested, of whom eight thousand were killed at Auschwitz. The remaining two thousand were married to "Aryans." The "Aryan" spouses, mostly women, gathered on the Rosen-strasse, where the Jews were incarcerated. The spouses began to shout: "Give us our husbands back!" They continued shouting for a week, day and night, even though they were informed by the guards that they would be shot if they did not disperse. The spouses would temporarily scramble, especially when shots were fired by the guards, but then they would reassemble and resume their shouting.

The Jews were released. Apparently Joseph Goebbels thought that this was the simplest way to end the protest. Although his diary reveals his desire to eventually rearrest the Jews, they were only forced to register with the police. In fact, they survived the war. And despite pressure from Nazi officials to divorce their Jewish spouses because of the alleged "racial shame" (*Rassenschande*) involved in such unions, the vast majority (93 percent) of "Aryans" married to Jews kept their marriages intact. Goebbels had to lie on May 19 when he said that Berlin was free of Jews (*judenfrei*). Heinrich Himmler responded similarly. On December 18, 1943, he ordered the deportation of Jews whose "Aryan" spouses had died or divorced them. But even some of these Jews were exempted if they had children who might cause unrest if they were deported.

(2) A second example concerns Nazi efforts to supplant the allegiance of many Germans to the Catholic Church. By late 1936 Nazi leaders were frustrated by the slow progress made in the effort to persuade Catholics to switch to the Nazi "faith." Hence they tried forcibly to replace Christian symbols with Nazi ones. On November 4 the Nazis ordered the removal of crucifixes from schools in the Cloppenburg district, which resulted in a storm of indignation among Catholics there. Priests supported the protests, which included ringing church bells every evening and sending children to school wearing crucifixes around their necks. This led to dissension within the Nazi ranks themselves, with some Nazi officials even aiding the protesters, or at least refusing to carry out the decree.

The Nazis backed down and retracted the decree. The "spirit of Cloppenburg" returned in April 1941, when Catholics again forced the retraction of a decree that crucifixes be removed in southern Germany (which is predominantly Catholic). Adolph Wagner, the Bavarian minister of education, issued the decree, which also included the stipulation that school prayer be dropped in favor of Nazi songs. Protests forced Wagner to rescind the decree after only two weeks. Angry crowds, mostly women, would yell, gather signatures on petitions, and so on. They also wrote their husbands fighting in the war, who were demoralized by the decree and supported their wives' efforts. Why fight godless communism if Germany itself was turning godless?

(3) Likewise, Hitler himself ordered a stop to "euthanasia," a Nazi euphemism for the murder by gassing of the deformed and insane. From January 1940 to August 1941, seventy thousand "undesirables" were killed. Hitler's order to stop these killings was, admittedly, intended to stop protests against these murders rather than the murders themselves, and an additional thirty thousand victims were killed in the remaining years of the Nazi regime, mostly forced laborers from the east (*Untermenschen*) who were not Germans. The cessation of the murders of deformed or insane Germans, however, was a direct consequence of forceful yet nonviolent popular opposition to such murders. This time, religious leaders, especially Catholic bishops, led the way from the pulpit. The Nazis soon realized, to their chagrin, that outspoken bishops like

Clemens August von Galen represented public opinion. An isolated individual, even a bishop, could be threatened into silence or thrown into jail, but when the public loved him, as they did von Galen, a more difficult challenge arose.

In short, the Nazis' racial hygiene program, which required the destruction of *lebensunwerten Lebens* (life unworthy of life), began to threaten popular support. That is, the cornerstone of Nazi politics (racial hygiene) threatened the cornerstone of Nazi power (popular support), to use Stoltzfus's terms. In July and August 1941, von Galen hammered away at the Gestapo from his pulpit in Münster, Westphalia. Fears were rising that soon even those injured in the war would become victims of the murder program. Goebbels and Hitler simply could not lose the support of the people; popular opinion thus not only protected von Galen but put an end to the murder of deformed or insane Germans. Once the issue was openly discussed, the murders had to stop.

In light of these three examples, several questions should be asked and several (albeit tentative) inferences should be drawn.

First, if nonviolent mass protests by "Aryan" Germans in 1943 prevented the murder of their Jewish spouses, could similar protests have slowed or stopped the destruction of other German Jews, or the destruction of Jews in general, as Stoltzfus suspects? Of course, counterfactual judgments regarding the past are a tricky business, as in Voltaire's query about whether history would have been radically altered had Cleopatra's nose been an inch longer. We will never know. But the question about the possible efficacy of nonviolent resistance to the Nazis has hardly been asked, much less answered adequately, and this is largely due to the prejudices of just war theorists/realists like Rawls.

Second, the available evidence seems to indicate that if a Jew was to be exempted from Nazi genocide, such an exemption depended on whether "Aryans" themselves were likely to make problems for the Nazis by compromising the secrecy of the Holocaust or by undermining civilian and combatant morale through protests. It should be remembered that the effort to wage total war is especially sensitive to challenges to patriotism, as when Hitler claimed in *Mein Kampf* that mass popular support was the distinguishing feature of the Nazis. In effect, if "Aryans" had cared for the Jews, even those Jews not favorably married to fellow "Aryans," history might have been radically altered, as in the case of Cleopatra's nose, contra Rawls and Walzer.

Third, in their resisting the replacement of crucifixes with swastikas, Catholic activists seemed to have been right that the regulations of the state would be ineffective if Catholics (and, by implication, Lutherans) stood together in resistance. In this case, even the clergy and the church hierarchy started to think in terms of collective nonviolent action against the Nazis.

Fourth, in the efforts to free the Jews married to "Aryans," as well as in the efforts to resist the removal of Christian symbols from schools, women took the lead. Here one is tempted to take seriously the possibility that previous efforts to rule out nonviolent resistance to the Nazis in principle were the result of male, or at least militaristic, bias. The efforts of the women who protested the removal of crucifixes, and of the women who demanded the release of their husbands, along with the efforts of Gandhi and Martin Luther King, point the way toward a consideration of this bias.

And fifth, J. P. Stern and Conor Cruise O'Brien may be right that if the Catholic Church had protested the Holocaust as energetically as it had protested the Nazi murder of the deformed and insane, then the "final solution" simply would not have occurred (see Stoltzfus 1992; Stern 1975).

Once again, I am well aware of the limited character of the claims that can be made as a result of the three examples given above. Further, I have not explored in any depth the likelihood that nonviolent resistance could have succeeded against Hitler and the Nazis if it had been practiced by non-Germans. This question would have to take seriously the resistance to the Nazis, very often nonviolent and very often efficacious, exhibited during the war in Denmark and Norway (Gjelsvik 1979; Petrow 1974). And it would also have to take seriously the nonviolent liberation of Poland and other countries in Eastern Europe from the Soviet Union in 1989, an example of a totalitarian power successfully resisted without war (Stokes 1993). But my aim here has also been minimal. It has been to call into question Rawls's (and Walzer's) assumption, still widely shared, that nonviolent resistance simply will not work with the likes of Hitler (or Stalin). It is the a priori nature of this assumption, which is contradicted by the scant evidence we have of nonviolent resistance to Hitler and the Nazis, that I find intellectually weak.

The point I would like to emphasize as a pacifist and a Rawlsian is that if democracy, or political liberalism broadly conceived, consists in trying to find peaceful modes of resolving disputes among those who hold different, even irreconcilably different, comprehensive religious or philosophical doctrines, then the resort to superior violence when confronted by Hitler indicates a partial collapse of democracy itself. That is, nonviolent resistance is not only a tactic or the expression of a sectarian religious conviction; it is also a defensible belief integrally connected to democratic or liberal political theory. The Western democracies, and not merely the Soviet Union, were not as democratic or as liberal as they could have been, in that in responding to Hitler and the Nazis through violence—indeed, through the bombing of cities as defended with qualification by Rawls and Walzer—they had to partially close the moral gap between their own theoretical commitment to resolving disputes fairly and nonviolently and the Nazi commitment to (savage) violence.

An interesting question arises about whether countries in the West that at least approximate just government will close the moral gap between themselves and countries that harbor terrorists. The pacifist's suggestion would be to encourage democratic governments to develop "greater conciliation," to use Taylor's phrase, on the analogy of the conciliatory economic policy urged by Keynes at the end of World War I. The bones of contention are familiar enough and are too complex to be analyzed here.

Perhaps an intelligent start to the process of reconciliation, from a pacifist point of view, lies in the observation that the way to win a "war" against terrorists who hide among the civilian population is to win over the minds and hearts of these civilian populations to political liberalism and democratic decision making (see White 2009). This victory would rob terrorists of their breeding grounds, just as a healthy Germany after World War I would have deprived the Nazis of theirs. And this victory, it seems, is predicated on convincing these populations that we in the West really care about Arabs and other peoples in the developing world for reasons other than the oil and cheap labor with which they provide us (see Lamb 1987). "Greater conciliation," rather than "appeasement," might very well make it more likely that Rawls's second and third original positions would be taken seriously at an international level. As Rawls himself notes (1999b, chapters 7–9), societies that are traditionally authoritarian or consultation hierarchies can change for the better and do not have to degenerate into outlaw states, especially if democracies treat them fairly and with respect.

In any event, I am not convinced that Rawlsians need to travel as far as Rawls himself did toward just war theory, much less toward realism.

I do not make this criticism easily. In light of Rawls's own personal experience as a soldier in one war and his experience opposing a later one, and given his status as the greatest political philosopher of the twentieth century, his views on war should certainly be taken seriously. But I am not convinced by those interpreters of Rawls who think that the power arrangements presupposed even in something as apparently pacific as voting have to be seen as implicit appeals to coercive power. Granted, there are outlaw states that are inherently aggressive and that are willing to go to war if it is in their interest to do so, but I hope that the examples given above indicate that there is more than one way to respond to such states.

I would like to close this chapter by coming to Rawls's defense against those critics who are entirely disappointed in his *Law of Peoples*. I think it is to Rawls's credit that he rejects a sort of liberal imperialism wherein politically liberal states are permitted or encouraged to impose liberal values on nonliberal states. As Lehning puts it, instructively, "Evidently, and contrary to Rawls's arguments, liberal imperialism is not seen by his [cosmopolitan] critics as problematic" (2009, 2–3, 5–6, 168, 178, 193, 240). It should be clear at this point why I *do* find liberal imperialism problematic. Indeed, liberal imperialism strikes me as a sort of crusade. As the cliché among religious pacifists has it, a willingness to die for the faith does not entail a willingness to kill for it.

3

NUSSBAUM, MENTAL DISABILITY,
AND ANIMAL ENTITLEMENTS:
A RAWLSIAN PERSPECTIVE

In several of Martha Nussbaum's recent writings she has expanded her concern for those historically left out of the male-dominated social contract (e.g., women, the mentally disabled) to include nonhuman animals (hereafter animals). Her own approach to animal entitlements is called "the capabilities approach," which both borrows from and rejects certain aspects of both a utilitarian approach to animals and a rights-based approach. But her stance regarding the relationship between social contract theory and animals is almost entirely negative; here there is no borrowing. Because she knows Rawls's thought well (indeed, her own political philosophy is heavily indebted to Rawls), but rejects his approach to both mentally deficient human beings and animals, Nussbaum provides an ideal frame for the present chapter. Through her we will be able to determine what is worth preserving and what should be rejected in a Rawlsian approach to mental disability and animality.

UTILITARIANISM

Nussbaum views Bentham as the first major modern philosophical theorist of animal entitlements. (It is curious that, as a classicist, she does not notice the contributions of the ancient Greeks in this regard [see Dombrowski 1984a, 1984b, 1984c, 1990, 2004b].) Bentham famously compared human treatment of animals to slavery, and he argued that our commonality with animals in suffering was *the* crucial topic in ethics. Nussbaum notes, however, that despite Bentham's opposition to sports that treated animals cruelly, he did not oppose meat eating (Nussbaum 2001a, 1522–26). The apparent anomaly here is due to certain complexities in utilitarian theory, she suggests.

On Nussbaum's interpretation, utilitarianism involves three key features: consequentialism (the right act is the one that produces the best consequences), sum-ranking (a theory regarding how to aggregate consequences across different lives), and a substantive view of the good. There are, she notes, two distinct versions of the utilitarian good. Bentham was a hedonistic utilitarian who asserted the supreme value of pleasure and the disvalue of pain, whereas contemporary utilitarians tend to defend preference-satisfaction utilitarianism, where the good is to further the *interests* of those affected by an action, whether or not those interests are hedonic.

There are problems with both utilitarian versions of the good, on Nussbaum's view, including familiar Rawlsian ones regarding the inability to rule out egregious harms if these have a positive aggregative effect. A second problem Nussbaum sees in utilitarian versions of the good concerns the claim that pleasures and pains, or preference satisfactions and dissatisfactions, are the only goods and bads. That is, even the updated preference-satisfaction version of utilitarianism (defended, say, by Peter Singer) is defective because on its basis there is nothing wrong with depriving a calf of free movement if it has never known a better way of life; the deprivation does not register on even a more expansive preference-satisfaction version of the utilitarian calculus. Third, all versions of utilitarianism are vulnerable regarding "the question of numbers," as in Singer's defense of the replaceability argument. According to this argument, if animals (and some marginal human beings?) are raised in humane conditions and are replaced with the same number of members of the same species, they can be killed with equanimity if the killing is painless (Dombrowski 2001b; also Singer 1979). What is bothersome in this argument, according to Nussbaum, is that individuals are viewed as replaceable containers of satisfactions rather than as ends in themselves who are capable of flourishing, and who desire to flourish, in their own unique ways.

There is a certain irony here. Despite the fact that Nussbaum's capabilities approach is, in general, closer to Rawlsian social contract theory than it is to utilitarianism (and this, in part, owing to the aforementioned problems Nussbaum sees in utilitarian versions of the good), her capabilities approach to animals, in particular, is closer to utilitarianism than it is to Rawlsian social contract theory. This rapprochement with utilitarianism is due to utilitarianism's skepticism about conventional morality, which historically has often ignored animals. That is, social contract theory in general has a tendency to treat all animals as strays who are outside the bounds of the contractors' original position, whereas utilitarianism gives them a home, or at least a shelter where they are safe for a while. Animal entitlements are ultimately not secure in utilitarianism because on this view animals are denied separateness, uniqueness, and inviolability. For example, Nussbaum thinks that the best reason to be against slavery of human beings or torture of animals is that these practices are violations of justice, not that they run afoul of empirical calculations of total/average well-being (2001a, 2004a, 2006, chapter 6).

The shortchanging of animal entitlements in utilitarianism does not seem to be primarily due, on Nussbaum's reasoning, to its consequentialism. Rather, it is due to (1) its versions of the good in terms of either pleasure or preference satisfaction, and (2) its conception of sum-ranking. It is difficult to sum-rank across species, she thinks, but despite this difficulty, there seems to be no way to rule out, on a utilitarian basis, great pain and cruel treatment of at least some animals. And we have seen Nussbaum claim that there are some things in life that are valuable other than pleasure, as in free movement, physical achievement, and altruistic sacrifice (2004a, 304). Nussbaum is correct to wonder if even preference-satisfaction utilitarianism (or Mill's pleasure-based utilitarianism, which allows for the existence of high-quality pleasures) can account for these. She asks, why *should* sentient beings seek out free movement, physical achievement, and why *should* they sometimes willingly accept altruistic sacrifice? Further, the preference-satisfaction utilitarian has to admit misinformed, malicious, or fear-induced preferences into the calculus, even pathological preferences that are the result of addiction. As before, animals are viewed by (even preference-satisfaction) utilitarians as replaceable containers of satisfactions with no convincing account offered for sum-ranking these satisfactions.

RIGHTS-BASED VIEWS

It is clear that Nussbaum has greater affinity with Tom Regan's rights-based view of animals (1983) than with Singer's utilitarian approach. A right, on Regan's view, is a pre-political valid ethical claim to certain treatment. Further, all moral agents (those whose conduct is morally assessable) *as well as* all moral patients (the wider class of those who suffer harms) have the right to respectful treatment. It should be noted that a "rights-based view" of animals is not a synonym in Nussbaum for "Kantian view" in that Kant thought (Rawls too?) that only moral agents have intrinsic value. If we have duties *regarding* animals in Kant's philosophy (not *to* them), these are indirect duties that are ultimately based on the direct duties we have to other rational human beings.

In addition to Regan, another rights-based view of animal entitlements is provided by Steven Wise, a legal scholar who tries to work animal rights into the existing common law framework (Wise 2000). Wise thinks that a necessary condition for animals to have legal rights is autonomy, albeit a realistic lower limit of autonomy possessed by chimpanzees who can think at the level of a three-year-old human being, including perspectival thinking where the world can be interpreted from another being's viewpoint. That is, some animals exhibit intellectual abilities, emotional sophistication, and autonomy to greater degrees than some human beings do, as in some cases of mental disability.

What are the strengths and weaknesses of the rights-based view, on Nussbaum's reasoning? One strength is the determination of rights-based theorists like Regan and Wise to view each animal as an end and an unwillingness to submit the interests of animals to a general utilitarian calculus. Second, rights-based views of animals do not have to be based solely on sentience, as do utilitarian views. For example, deprivation of liberty or bodily integrity can count as evils on rights-based views, even if they do not register in the creature's awareness or in the utilitarian calculus.

But Nussbaum sees two problems with rights-based views of animals, problems to which I will return below. The first is that rights-based views are overly insistent regarding moral egalitarianism, she thinks. Although Nussbaum admits that the species barrier itself is of no moral relevance, she thinks that morally relevant traits "may often be correlated with species membership" (2001a, 1534). Presumably what she has in mind is the idea that, although being a member of the human species is not in itself morally relevant (with species membership in biology referring merely to being in a breeding population), the fact that human beings typically have several high-level capabilities for autonomy and rational thought *is* morally relevant. In this regard Nussbaum thinks that Singer is closer to the truth than Regan because Regan is more firmly committed to the moral irrelevance of species membership. The other problem with rights-based views of animal entitlements, according to Nussbaum, is that rights in general are "a little loose and vague" unless they are "incorporated into an ethical approach that spells out the basis for rights" (1535). In effect, rights are defensible only when they are seen in the broader (neo-Aristotelian) context of the capabilities approach.

CRITICISMS OF SOCIAL CONTRACT THEORY

Rawls thinks that duties of justice are based on the idea of reciprocity. And he assumes that animals are incapable of reciprocity. As a result, Nussbaum concludes that we have no duties of justice to animals on a contractarian basis. If we ought to be compassionate to animals, as Rawls seems to admit, such compassion is nonetheless outside the scope of *justice*. Perhaps the duty to be compassionate is an indirect duty similar to the one found in the Stoics, Saint Thomas Aquinas, and Kant: we have duties *regarding* animals but not *to* them, as in the duty not to torture animals because violation of this duty makes it more likely that we would torture (reciprocating) human beings. In any event, compassion regarding animals is not part of "the basic structure" of society in social contract theory.

Nussbaum finds this approach inadequate for several reasons. Most notably, social contract theorists postpone animal entitlements until a later stage of politics after the basic structure is in place, in effect leaving the issue for politicians and judges to deal with, not political philosophers dealing with duties of justice at the most abstract level. This would be an abdication of responsibility, Nussbaum correctly notes. Further, she thinks that by identifying citizens with their mental and moral powers, not with their animal bodies, social contract theorists in the Kantian tradition of moral philosophy, especially Rawls, separate human dignity from the natural (animal) world. "The idea that at bottom we are split beings," she points out, "both rational persons and animal dwellers in the world of nature, never ceases to influence Kant's way of thinking. . . .

Rawls seems to adopt this way of thinking" (2001a, 1528; 2004a, 301; see also Scanlon 1998, 177–87, 221). One is reminded here of the familiar Marxist charge that behind Kant lies Christianity, with its denigration of animal bodies (see Goldmann 1971). Whether religious believers in general or Christian believers in particular have really had such a negative view of our animal bodies is open to dispute, however (see Brown 1988).

This alleged split fails to account for the fact that we human beings are dignified *as* animals, and it encourages us to think of ourselves as self-sufficient in the sense that we could (at least imaginatively) identify ourselves as noumenal selves completely lacking animality, something like disembodied cogitos outside of time and stripped of the animal (specifically mammal) dependencies that are essential parts of the human life cycle, especially in infancy and in cases of mental disability. That is, Nussbaum accuses social contract theorists, especially Rawls, of distorting the intimate (Aristotelian, hylomorphic) connection between rationality and the well-being of our animal bodies. To be urged to care about rationality without being urged to care about our animality, she thinks, leaves us with an inadequate basis for thinking about our needs, including what Rawls would call our needs for primary goods. In sum, recognizing "greater continuity between humans and other animals may actually be essential for thinking well about ourselves" (Nussbaum 2001a, 1529; 2001b, 37–38; 2006, 159, 356).

Despite Nussbaum's affinity in many other respects with Rawls's political liberalism, she thinks that it fails miserably regarding animals. We will see that she need not be so pessimistic regarding social contract theory. Once again, the point is not to develop a more positive view of animal entitlements so as to compete with Nussbaum's capabilities approach, but to complement her approach from a social contract point of view. I assume that, because of her own political liberalism, Nussbaum would welcome a more friendly connection between her capabilities approach and a Rawlsian approach to animal entitlements, but she is skeptical about any strong connection because of the implausibility of there being any contract between rational human beings and animals, primarily owing to the asymmetry of *power* between the two. Nussbaum seems to conflate here the Rawlsian social contract and the Hobbesian one, the latter of which depends on each party's threat advantage in a state of nature. This is a mistake, I think, but Nussbaum's bigger error is to think of animals in a social contract context as (deficient) moral agents rather than as (robust) moral patients, as we will see (Nussbaum 2004a, 300–302).

AN ANIMAL-FRIENDLY VERSION OF SOCIAL CONTRACT THEORY

I will assume that the reader is familiar with two basic arguments commonly used by defenders of animal entitlements, including, in a way, Nussbaum. The first of these is the argument from sentiency, which, in abbreviated form, suggests that it is morally wrong to do avoidable harm to a sentient being who is capable of being harmed; yet such avoidable harm is done routinely to animals when they are seen as sources of food, clothing, and so on; thus it is morally wrong to use them in these ways.

The second argument is that from marginal cases, which, again in abbreviated form, suggests that Rawlsian reasonableness/rationality is not a defensible criterion for moral patiency in that it would exclude many human beings (the marginal cases of humanity) from the class of moral patients, thereby making it possible (obviously contra Rawls's intention) to eat infantburgers or, more plausibly, to experiment painfully or lethally on mentally deficient humans. If the marginal cases have rights, however (as Nussbaum rightly thinks they do), then the same basic rights should be granted to those animals who are at equivalent levels of morally relevant criteria like cognitive and affective abilities, especially the ability to be harmed or pained. That is, the argument from marginal cases can just as easily be referred to as the argument for moral consistency if the phrase "marginal cases" is found objectionable. To avoid the argument, as Rawls tries to do, by, in effect, claiming that nonrational yet sentient human beings deserve moral respect (see, e.g., Rawls 2001, 176), but that animals, who are nonrational yet sentient, do not, because they *are* human beings, is to resort to speciesism. This is a type of arbitrariness like classism, racism, and sexism, which both Nussbaum and Rawls should want to avoid.

The approach I am taking here is different from that of Freeman, who thinks that those mentally deficient human beings who are not capable of high-level cooperation with reasonable/rational human beings are not the recipients of distributive *justice*, although he does admit that they can be the recipients of actions performed by those who have natural duties. A partial response to Freeman consists in pointing out that there are clearly other examples of Rawlsian justice that do not require reciprocity, as in duties of justice to members of future generations, who do not exactly cooperate with us, despite Freeman's locution regarding treating them as we would want them to treat us (time-travel?). Freeman, as the father of an autistic child, and I, as the father of an adopted son who is developmentally delayed, no doubt agree in practice about how human beings outside of the norm ought to be treated (see Freeman 2007b, 272). But I have a different sense of how Rawlsian theory ought to go regarding nonparadigmatic human beings and nonhuman animals so as to avoid the extensive criticism Rawls has received on these topics (see Freeman 2007b, 106–9, 138–39, 271–72).

It seems to me that Freeman is too lenient on Rawls when he cites only Rawls's claim in *A Theory of Justice* (Rawls 1999c, 442) that having the moral powers is a sufficient condition to warrant equal justice, but not a necessary one. In an earlier essay, from 1963, Rawls makes the dangerous claim that having the moral powers is a necessary condition for warranting equal justice (Rawls 1999a, 99). This puts the marginal cases of humanity in theoretical peril, as I see things. Further, when Freeman says that all human beings deserve moral respect because they *are* human beings, he both begs the question, I think, and slips into speciesist thinking. To reiterate: both Rawls and Freeman think that the marginal cases of humanity, or nonparadigmatic human beings (or whatever label is most appropriate for human beings who fail to meet the threshold of reasonableness/rationality required to deliberate in the original position), ought to be protected and treated with care and consideration (see Freeman 2007b, 286–88). But why?

There are three ways in which one could develop a more marginal case–friendly and animal-friendly social contract view than the one found in Rawls's own writings (Dombrowski 1998, 2001a). The first concerns the room available within the concept of natural duty to defend the argument from sentiency. The concept of natural duty becomes understandable when we realize that it is redundant to have reasonable contractors promise not to murder each other. We need the reasonable contract for the difficult cases. It is crucial to notice that Rawls himself lists among our natural duties the duty not to harm or injure another and the duty not to cause unnecessary suffering. In fact, these two negative duties are, according to Rawls, stronger than any positive natural duties we might have. These natural duties apply without regard to our voluntary acts, as in those found in the original position, and without regard to our institutional relationships (Rawls 1999c, 98–99; also van Parijs 2003, 239–40;

Daniels 2003, 257–59; Nussbaum 2003, 511–15; Cureton 2008; Kittay 1997). These features are what suggest the propriety of the adjective "natural," a designation that would presumably be acceptable to Nussbaum as well.

If there is a natural duty not to cause unnecessary suffering, it makes sense to suggest that this duty applies to all beings who have the capacity to suffer, to all beings, say, with central nervous systems. Or again, there is some textual evidence to suggest that Rawls thinks that animals ought not to be treated cruelly (as Nussbaum notices) even though they are not themselves bound by the natural duty not to be cruel (Rawls 1999c, 448). Why not also say that animals ought to be treated justly even if they are not duty bound to be just?

Second, it is possible to argue in favor of a revised original position, which is more favorable to the idea of animal entitlements than the original original position—not a redundancy (Vandeveer 1979; Regan 1981; Elliot 1984; Huffman 1993; Rowlands 1997; cf. Fuchs 1981; Russow 1992). That is, the original position should be reconceived. Even if we assume that only reasonable/rational human beings can inhabit the original position, this does not necessarily mean that only they can be incarnated when the veil of ignorance is lifted. The veil of ignorance needs to be thicker so as to occlude vision not only of one's race, class, and sex but also of one's species. The reason for this thicker veil is that animals have individual welfare in the sense that their experiential lives can go well or ill for them. At the very least, they can be treated cruelly, as Rawls himself admits. The argument from marginal cases can be used to supplement Rawls, in that many marginal human beings whom Rawls wants to protect by decisions made in the original position no more possess moral agency than do most higher animals (i.e., those with central nervous systems).

In the revised original position we can identify principles that would reasonably adjudicate conflicting claims among all sentient creatures. Remember that parties in the original position must assume that they could turn out to be among the least intellectually advantaged human beings, which could be seen to imply that they might even turn out to be severely mentally deficient. Even if only a small percentage of the human population fails to have moral agency (a sense of justice and a rational plan of life), we are dealing with a significant number of people, perhaps tens of millions of them: anencephalic infants, the seriously psychotic, a subset of Down syndrome cases, the severely mentally deficient, the senile, the irreversibly comatose, and so on. There is no reason to think that Rawls would deny that we have duties of *some* sort to such beings, and he explicitly says that it would be unwise in practice to withhold treatment from them (see Vandeveer 1979, 368–77).

If one says that we ought to extend just treatment to marginal cases even though they are not owed it, we are obviously left with a puzzle. A more efficacious way to deal with the matter is to say that justice involves duties to those sentient yet nonrational human beings who are not moral agents, as well as to sentient yet nonrational animals who are not moral agents. Participants in the original position should choose principles for all beings with interests, or better, for all beings concerning whom we can speak of *their own* well-being or ill-being. Rawls's own (apparent) natural duty not to be cruel to animals seems to imply this. To choose in favor of marginal cases but not animals solely on the basis of species membership is to be speciesist, a failing that is analogous to being classist, racist, or sexist. Vandeveer puts the matter this way: "If, then, the original position were fully neutral, its participants would not only have to be ignorant of [their] race, sex, or social position qua participants [in the just society], it would seem that they would have to be ignorant of their species membership as well—subject only to the qualification that they shall have interests as participants [in the just society]. This version of the original position is not that of Rawls. Yet . . . it is not clear why it ought not to be" (1979, 372–73). That is, we should not assume, as Nussbaum does, that Rawls was the best interpreter regarding the implications of his own theory of justice for animals.

If we knew we were to be incarnated as white or black, racist principles would more likely be chosen in the original position than if we did not have this knowledge. Likewise, if we assumed that we would be incarnated as human beings, speciesist principles would more likely be chosen than if we did not have this knowledge. If, however, we assume that we might each be incarnated as a sentient, nonrational being (of whatever species), it would be reasonable in the original position to insist on duties to such a being, provided such a being posed no serious threat to others. It does not help much to respond by saying that animals do not even have the possibility of becoming moral agents when we realize that permanently mentally disabled or senile human beings do not have this possibility, either, as Nussbaum would no doubt admit. But this revised original position is still compatible with due attention being paid to the more sophisticated interests of reasonable/rational beings.

There is something inadequate about the following claim, a claim that is at least hinted at by Rawls and made explicit by other contract theorists and implied by Nussbaum: the human species is deemed uniquely morally significant because its members *typically* are moral agents with a sense of justice. But this is precisely speciesism, in that the characteristics of individual animals and human beings are ignored: "If we start down the road of including beings within our scope of moral concern simply because they are members of some group or another, we may just as easily *exclude* others because of their group membership. This strategy is, of course, typical of racism, sexism, and all of the other 'isms' that seek to assign individuals more or less value than others based on their membership in some group" (Huffman 1993, 22). The proper task for parties in the revised original position is to protect any individual with a makeup sufficiently sophisticated to allow it to suffer pain or harm. Even if such an individual might not be a moral agent, there is nothing that logically prevents it from being a moral patient. It is quite common for us to enter into a contract for the sake of another who is not a moral agent, as in a contract with a day-care center or a home for the mentally disabled, as Nussbaum would again no doubt admit.

The interests of sentient yet nonrational beings could, and indeed should, be considered in the original position, despite what Nussbaum assumes about the original position. Those in the original position are rational and mutually disinterested, but Rawls himself implies that they might not have these qualities to any great extent when they are incarnated. The one restriction on the scope of this incarnation is that the being in question can benefit from the decisions made by the rational and mutually disinterested parties in the original position: marginal cases and animals can so benefit; rocks and insects and plants (presumably) cannot, as Rawls himself seems to admit. An example from fiction is helpful. In *Flowers for Algernon,* by Daniel Keyes, a severely mentally deficient man is made temporarily rational (in fact, a genius) by a miracle drug that eventually wears off. We can easily imagine the demands he would make while rational regarding how he would like to be treated when the drug wears off. It should not be too hard to do the same were the subject in question a chimpanzee, a cow, or a laboratory mouse (Huffman 1993, 26; Rawls 1999c, 354).

Third, in addition to the existence of natural duties and the possibility of a revised original position, a defense of animal entitlements can be found in various comprehensive doctrines that citizens hold in a liberal democracy. That is, what we agree to in the original position will most probably be far less than what is included in our own comprehensive view, in that what we are looking for in the social contract is an overlapping consensus that can be reached with those who have views that, although reasonable and comprehensive, differ, sometimes uncompromisingly, from our own. In fact, it is the existence of reasonable pluralism of comprehensive religious, philosophical, or moral views that creates the need for a social contract and public reason, as Nussbaum would seem to agree. And Rawls himself acknowledges the existence of, and wants to remove barriers to the flourishing of, a comprehensive view that defends animal entitlements (he calls it the view of "natural religion" [1996, 20–21, 245–46, 272]).

It must be admitted that Rawls also acknowledges the existence of traditional (Judeo-Christian) anthropocentrism, which he sees in contrast to natural religion. This latter view he identifies as a stewardship view. To adopt the stewardship view of natural religion, he thinks, is not a constitutional essential or a basic question of justice as these questions are specified in the original position; public reason does not apply to the concern for animals shown by the natural religionist. Natural religionists are nonetheless free to try to convince other citizens of their (nonpolitical) views, he admits.

The question to be asked of Rawls, however, is whether the traditional Judeo-Christian view of animals that he apparently admires is to be identified as a constitutional essential or a basic matter of justice any more than is the stewardship view he apparently rejects. Rawls's strong anthropocentrism, which partially overlaps with Nussbaum's own qualified anthropocentrism, as we will see, is a feature of his view that would be compatible with the original version of the original position, but not with the revised version (Rawls cites Thomas 1983; Freeman 2007b, 81, is like Rawls in this regard in that animal sacrifices would be permitted as long as there were no human health risks involved).

The important thing is to avoid the conclusion, apparently endorsed by Freeman, that utilitarianism has an insider's advantage in the effort to deal adequately with animal suffering, and perhaps with the suffering of disabled human beings, because of the tight connection between utilitarian morality and a view of the ultimate good in terms of pleasurable consciousness (see Freeman 2007a, 59–60). Granted, Rawls himself may have thought of the participants in the original position and the beneficiaries of the decisions made there as both involving moral agency of at least a minimal sort, such that the prime recipients of the difference principle would be reasonable/rational minimum-wage workers rather than those human beings with severe mental or physical disabilities. But this interpretation of the original position leads to the enormous problems Nussbaum emphasizes (cf. Freeman 2007a, 125–27). We should not infer from this, however, that the problems are integral to social contract theory itself, as the revised original position articulated above indicates.

It is frustrating to see Freeman follow Rawls by relegating their obvious concern for both animals and mentally disabled human beings to some region either outside of justice or at least outside of that part of justice for which Rawls is most famous and most insightful: the deliberations of reasonable/rational agents in an original position of ignorance. Granted, the natural duty not to be cruel is a help, as is the advice received from some (but not all) comprehensive doctrines regarding how to treat animals and nonparadigmatic human beings. But more needs to be said, and the revised original position (seemingly rejected by Rawls and Freeman) enables us to say it. Even if it is true that the difference principle focuses initially on production and not on consumption (with animals and nonparadigmatic humans being nonproducers), an adequate theory of justice would have to address fully, rather than tangentially, those who have consumption needs but through no fault of their own are unable to produce (see Freeman 2007a, 204, 264, 294, 319).

No doubt I will receive the criticism that to include mentally deficient human beings and animals in the class of moral patients is to concern ourselves with the justice of the universe and not merely with the justice of our own social institutions. If this were correct, then we would be dealing with theodicy or some other topic in philosophy of religion rather than with political philosophy. My reply is that in the original position this distinction would be hard to maintain in that it is precisely the worst possible cases, the most egregious forms of suffering, that we ought to think about. To, in effect, legislate out of existence the suffering of mentally deficient human beings or animals is both to beg the question in favor of (rational) anthropocentrism and to merely stipulate that justice is species-bound (see Pogge 2007, x, 39, 44, 63, 74, 77, 88).

ANIMAL EMOTIONS

The Rawl*sian* use of the argument from marginal cases in the revised original position is certainly compatible with Nussbaum's implicit use of this argument, wherein the language of capabilities enables us to "move beyond the species barrier" in order to see dignity in our own animal faculties. Seeing this dignity enables us to deal better, she thinks, with issues regarding mental disability and old age, issues that already affect others directly and could affect us directly in the future. And dealing better with the marginal cases of humanity enables us, via the argument from marginal cases, to deal better with animals. That is, even though Nussbaum is not as insistent on the absolute irrelevance of species membership as some advocates of animal rights are, she does, in general, see such membership as irrelevant: "a right may be qualified in certain ways in keeping with the creature's level of understanding" (2001a, 1538, 1548; 2004a, 306–7).

Nussbaum is aware that there are two distinct uses of the argument from marginal cases, and that only one of them is defensible. Once we do away with the sharp moral dichotomy between human beings and animals, we might start to treat animals humanely, the way we now (for the most part) treat marginal cases of humanity—the defensible version of the argument. It is also possible, however, that we would start to treat marginal cases of humanity the way we now treat animals. Although it is not likely that this (indefensible) version of the argument from marginal cases would increase the populations of marginal human beings treated as commodities in the slaughterhouse, it might increase the number of research subjects in biomedical research laboratories. This is why it is important to think carefully about the revised original position and about natural duty so as to secure the rights of the marginal cases of humanity on a contractarian basis (Nussbaum 2001a, 1521–22; cf. Frey 1983, 115–16).

Defense of the argument from marginal cases is facilitated by one of Nussbaum's most recent books, which includes a carefully documented chapter titled "Humans and Other Animals," where animal psychology is treated in detail. Here Nussbaum rejoices in the decline of reductionist (and behaviorist) theories of emotion; this decline enables us to see emotions as richly cognitive phenomena. Both human beings and animals have emotions that involve intentionality, selective attention, and appraisal. Animals often get angry because they are *given reason to be* angry.

Or again, emotions (e.g., grief) are appraisals wherein an animal sees that one of its goals is at stake. If a rich cognitive life is *not* ascribed to animals, animal behavior itself is hard, if not impossible, to explain. To say that an emotion is cognitive, however, is not to say that it entails a sophisticated self-consciousness or reflectivity, only that it involves the conscious processing of information. Nevertheless, because many of the goals of animals are eudaemonistic, with various emotions indicating progress toward, or regress away from, attainment of these goals, emotions contain an indexical element, at least in the sense that they involve *some* awareness that it is herself or himself who has the goal (Nussbaum 2001c, 89–118).

Relying on George Pitcher, Nussbaum attributes emotions with propositional content to animals. That is, an emotion is an evaluative *appraisal* of the world; there is something the world is like to an animal with an emotion. For example, a dog who has been beaten by a human being, but who then comes into contact with a different human being who is kind and who repeatedly offers a biscuit, reacts initially with fear and reticence but then eventually with a wagging tail. Pitcher (and Nussbaum) attribute something like the following to the dog's way of thinking: "Most human beings are to be avoided, but this human being is different." This Nussbaumian view of emotion as involving appraisal of the world helps us to distinguish emotional "pulls" from simpler appetites or "pushes" like hunger (Nussbaum 2001c, 119–38; Pitcher 1965, 326–46; 1995).

Rapprochement between Rawlsian social contract theory and Nussbaum on animals can be reached thanks to the revised original position (Dombrowski 1997a) *and* to the nuanced theory of animal emotion developed by Nussbaum herself. Unfortunately, Rawls largely uses a meat-cleaver approach: human beings are reasonable/rational contractors; animals are not. But we have seen that many human beings are not reasonable/rational contractors, and that many animals have emotions that involve intentionality, selective attention, and appraisal. Of course, Nussbaum's view of animal emotions is perfectly compatible with the stance that there are important differences between animals and those human beings who *are* capable of reasonableness/rationality. Temporal thinking, she admits, is limited in animals (although the aforementioned dog who was beaten as a puppy has *some* sense of what has happened in the past and a desire not to have it repeated in the future). As a result of this limitation, animal capacity for generalization is more limited than in a reasonable/rational human being. Although most animals have a general notion of "food," presumably they are not aware of historical patterns of oppression, or even of the concept "being abused in puppyhood."

The point is a subtle one. Capacity to generalize is related to the capacity to engage in perspectival thinking, which, although limited in animals, is nonetheless found in a greater degree in many animals (especially in chimpanzees) than in some autistic children. In the effort to bring together Nussbaum's capabilities approach to animals and Rawlsian social contract theory, it is interesting to note that although animals are limited in the degree to which they can engage in reciprocal relations, this limitation is nonetheless subject to the argument from marginal cases: their limitation is continuous with, and sometimes is less than, comparable limitation in some human beings. It would be exceedingly difficult to deny reciprocity altogether to apes who have learned American Sign Language and dogs who guide the blind. That is, although the revised original position concentrates on animals as moral patients, it would be a mistake to view moral agency in a meat-cleaver, all-or-nothing way (Nussbaum 2001c, 144–51; 1999, 72, 258; Anderson 2004; cf. Dombrowski 2006b).

I would like to make it explicit, however, that I very much agree with Nussbaum's (and Anderson's) point that once the minimal rights that the argument from marginal cases affords to mentally deficient human beings and to animals are acknowledged, it is permissible, perhaps required, to acknowledge additional protections and capabilities regarding mentally deficient human beings due to certain species-specific capabilities. Consider what might seem a trivial example, but one that I think is quite serious: cleanliness. Pigs like to roll in the mud for various reasons: it helps them to cool off, to get rid of insects, and so on. But although mentally deficient human beings might not mind if they live in filth (their own or others'), they have a species-specific right to have their hygiene needs attended to by competent others.

In short, although species membership may not be relevant when considering the minimum requirement (sentiency) of moral patiency status itself, this does not prevent the consideration of additional species-dependent properties that deserve our attention. Analogously, once basic rights are protected for all human beings, there is no reason to prohibit additional duties being placed on our shoulders with respect to our friends and relatives.

THE CAPABILITIES APPROACH

The general theoretical compatibility of Nussbaum's capabilities approach and Rawlsian social contract theory is found in Nussbaum's belief that once needs for primary goods are fulfilled, human beings should be free to pursue any perfectionistic goods they wish that are compatible with justice. Her view is at once Aristotelian and Rawlsian. Each creature strives for a good, but for human beings to become fully human they must avoid realities that stunt their capabilities.

Nussbaum's list of central human capabilities is developed in several of her recent writings and includes life, bodily health, bodily integrity, education, emotion, practical reason, affiliation, social basis for self-respect, and so on, as well as the capacity "to live with concern for and in relation to animals, plants, and the world of nature" (2001a, 1536). This is a list of capabilities, not actual functionings. The politically liberal point is to avoid "dragooning" beings into functioning in a certain way, in that Nussbaum explicitly identifies her view with Rawls's own regarding individuals as ends in themselves. The main difference is that she does not agree with Rawls's split between human beings and animals. As before, when such a split is avoided we are better equipped as emotional/intelligent animals, rather than as supposed disembodied cogitos or noumenal selves, to deal with humans with mental disabilities and other animals.

The "obvious and intimate relation" between Nussbaum's (neo-Aristotelian) capabilities approach and approaches like Rawls's own is reinforced by the language of rights so as to emphasize justified claims regarding the capabilities in the list given above. Further, Nussbaum, along with James Rachels, is a "moral individualist" in the sense that although species membership is frequently a good shortcut to identifying certain relevant needs and capabilities, it is not always so when individual differences within or across species boundaries are considered. This *should be* Rawls's view as well. Despite Nussbaum's (unfortunate) reticence about defending vegetarianism on a philosophical basis, she is nonetheless to be commended for making explicit that the capabilities view "would give all animals entitlements in the areas of life, bodily integrity, and some relevant types of dignity and liberty" (2001a, 1543; see also Rachels 1990).

It is because many basic human capabilities are shared with animals that Nussbaum is confident in claiming that her approach can more easily be extended to include animals than other prominent theories can.

This is true despite the fact that her theory starts by considering human beings. Past failures to educate blacks and women are at least analogous to a failure to allow an animal a good life: all three are kinds of "premature death." To those who might be offended by comparing human beings to animals (it is to be remembered that human beings are not *like* animals; they *are* animals), Nussbaum suggests a quotation from Aristotle: "If there is anyone who thinks it is base to study animals, he should have the same thought about himself" (*Parts of Animals* 645A).

Nussbaum's sense of the relationship between the capabilities approach (including the capabilities approach as it relates to animals) and Rawlsian social contract theory is worthy of our consideration because the capabilities approach does not operate with a fully comprehensive conception of the good. This is due to the respect one should have for the various ways in which people live their lives in a pluralistic society. The capabilities approach aims at securing some core entitlements that are implicit in the idea of a life with dignity; hence it focuses on a relatively small list. But human beings also affect in a dramatic way animals' opportunities for flourishing. Therefore, we need laws designed for the protection of animals. (If human beings had not so pervasively interfered with animals' ways of life, the most respectful strategy might have been, at least with respect to wild animals, to leave them alone [see Nussbaum 2004a, 307–17].) These moral duties to, and laws concerning, animals take individual animals, not species, as their locus. This is comparable to Rawls's deontological commitment to individuals rather than to the aggregative logic of utilitarianism (Nussbaum 2004a, 307).

But these individuals have different levels of complexity and hence different levels of capability. Nussbaum sees her view here as contrasting with that of Regan, to whom she attributes the belief that all who have intrinsic value (actually Regan says inherent value) have it equally. In effect, Nussbaum is making it clear that rabbits, say, are not to be given the right to vote, nor are they to be seen as reasonable/rational agents who could participate in the original position. It makes sense to distinguish in some fashion or other between lower animals (amoebas, mosquitoes, shrimp) and higher animals (rabbits, fish, pigs), with the higher ones having intellectual abilities and affective traits that may very well be inferior to those of normal reasonable/rational human beings but which are nonetheless continuous with, or may even exceed, those of many other human beings (Nussbaum 2004a, 308–9; 1995, 79, 82, 106; 1999, 362).

This admission of animals, at least the higher ones, as moral patients, as recipients of decisions made in the revised original position, but a certain skepticism regarding (rather than a refusal to consider) animals as moral agents, serves to fend off the familiar charge that animal rightists romanticize animals. Nature is brutal, as Nussbaum rightly emphasizes along with Mill (see his "Nature"). This judgment is not exclusively due to anthropocentric interests to avoid predators and cancer cells; it is also due to contemporary ecology (Callicott 1989). As Nussbaum sees things, respect for nature (including animal nature) does not mean just leaving nature as it is. It must involve careful normative arguments about what appropriate goals might be. One place to begin is with the best evidence we have regarding what animals do when left to their own devices (Nussbaum 2004a, 310–11). On this subject Nussbaum insightfully shows the complexity of the standard way of understanding the distinction between negative and positive duties, a distinction reinforced by Rawls, at least at the level of natural duty (Rawls 1999c, 98; Nussbaum 2004a, 312–13).

It has been traditionally assumed not only that there is a distinction between negative and positive duties but that the former have priority over the latter. For example, it has been assumed that it is obviously wrong to harm another by aggression but that letting people die of hunger might be morally permissible. The capabilities approach calls this judgment into question; on the basis of this view, part of a person's holdings that are needed by others whose really basic needs are not being met are really owned by the people who need them, not by those who are hoarding them (Nussbaum 2004a, 312–13). In this regard Nussbaum's view is like that of Saint Thomas Aquinas. But Nussbaum thinks that there might still be room for maintaining the distinction between negative and positive duties in regard to animals. First, by *not* harming them, we give them a chance to flourish in their own way; we ought not to be despots (not even benevolent ones) who control the minutiae of the world. But second, the priority of negative duties over positive ones cannot be accepted *in full* even with regard to animals because huge numbers of animals *do* live under direct human control, and because we affect the habitats of those in the wild. Here we have positive duties.

The question of how much we should do *for* wild animals is analogous, it seems, to the question of how much foreign aid to give. In neither case do we want to foster dependency; we do not want to turn wild animals into semi-domesticated ones. Further, by "wild animals" we should mean both predator and prey, such that for the former to flourish some of the latter can be expected to suffer and die. Given our miserable history of wildlife "management," it is by no means clear that we would or could make things better by altogether preventing predation in the wild. Admittedly there is a tension here: the Rawlsian distinction between negative and positive duties (and the priority of the former) would promote a more laissez-faire attitude toward animals in the wild, whereas Nussbaum's capabilities approach would encourage us to protect prey in the wild *so long as* we did not prevent the predator from flourishing. And, it should be noted, it is predators rather than prey who have had a rougher time of it with the destruction of wilderness. Nussbaum comes at this very difficult issue by suggesting that predation may be a less painful death than death by famine or disease. It makes sense that we have less responsibility to protect deer than we do to protect domestic animals, since we are the caretakers of the latter. But if we could protect wild animals without the kind of intrusive intervention that would produce negative consequences over the long haul, then Nussbaum could be persuaded that we ought to do so. The capabilities of predatory animals need to be considered along with those of prey, but we do not have the alternative of giving the tiger in the wild a nice ball on a string to play with, an alternative that makes sense with respect to domestic cats, who are also predators (Nussbaum 2004a, 310–13; Palmer 2010).

In any event, Nussbaum thinks that the distinction between negative and positive duties cannot be maintained *in its classical form* in the case of animals. Humans constantly intervene with animals; the question is what shape this intervention should take. Even paternalism (if it is respectful) can be better than harmful neglect (Nussbaum 2004a, 317–18). Once again, however, as with her refusal to defend philosophical vegetarianism, it is easy to detect in Nussbaum's thought an unfortunate backsliding away from a steadfast defense of animal entitlements (see also Hare 1999, 233–46).

It is not the case, as Nussbaum alleges, that contract theorists *necessarily* have difficulty, as Rawls himself sometimes does, in distinguishing between the questions "Who are the subjects of justice?" and "Who are the makers of a theory of justice?" The revised original position makes precisely this distinction. On the basis of this distinction a Rawls*ian* defender of animal entitlements like myself could agree with most of the implications of Nussbaum's capabilities approach as they relate to animals. For example, I agree with Nussbaum that animals are entitled to *life.* The difficulty I have with her view is not that she takes a neo-Aristotelian capabilities approach, but rather that she assumes (along with Hare) that if animals were killed in a painless fashion *after* a healthy free-ranging life, then there would be no problem. She should check with fellow meat eaters, however, to see if they are willing to eat flesh that is on the verge of being carrion. It is the flesh of animals in their prime that most meat eaters want and that the Food and Drug Administration will approve. Further, and more important, Nussbaum's willingness to kill and eat animals conflicts with her aforementioned defense of the view that animals are not chips in a utilitarian calculus but are ends in themselves (2004a, 315, 318).

The other capabilities Nussbaum lists are also compatible with, in fact are helpful additions to, the existing literature on animal entitlements. Especially noteworthy are capabilities regarding bodily health, bodily integrity (e.g., where castration, as opposed to sterilization, of an animal is cruel), education (e.g., the border collie who is trained to herd sheep is not necessarily abused), emotions (especially the capacity for love and care for conspecifics and housemates—animals are or can become "affiliated" with others, even the supposedly "lone" wolf), play, and so on. What we want is an interdependent world where not only different peoples but also members of different animal species engage in mutually supportive relations with one another so that animal flourishing is not the exception to the rule. This interdependent world, attentive to the particular needs of predators, is a partial supplanting of the natural by the just, somewhat in agreement and somewhat in disagreement with Mill (Nussbaum 2004a, 319; 1999, 41).

Conflict cannot be eliminated, on Nussbaum's view, informed as it is by her long experience with the Greek tragedians (Nussbaum 1986). The focus, she thinks, should be on long-term planning that will help us to create a social world (and, I assume, to accept appropriately a wild world) "in which all the capabilities can be secured to all citizens" (including, I assume, animal "citizens"). Aristotelian moderation is called for: neither utopian fantasies nor anesthetic accommodation to present injustices. This is very Rawlsian in theory, given Rawls's defense of "realistic utopia" (1999b). Regrettably, Nussbaum, like Rawls, too easily accommodates her thinking to existing injustices and cruelties inflicted on animals, not merely medical experimentation on animals, where tragic choices must be made, she thinks (along with Singer), but also regarding the table. Philosophical vegetarians like myself, however, claim to have strong arguments that lead us to see that meat eating is closer to cosmetics testing (which Nussbaum largely, but not entirely, rejects) than it is to painful and lethal testing on animals that may result in cures for diseases that afflict human beings (Nussbaum 2004a, 315–19; 2001c, 101, 118; 2000a).

Nussbaum commends Rawls and the liberal social contract tradition for dealing well with unfair inequalities among human beings, both nationally and to at least some extent internationally. The most unsatisfactory aspect of this tradition, she thinks, is its historical failure to deal well with distribution of opportunities within the family, with the mentally disabled, and with animals. It is my purpose in this chapter to try to eliminate the last two of these three admitted deficiencies. Further, Nussbaum is correct to insist that the capabilities approach can help us to push forward regarding all three, commendably providing in a neo-Aristotelian way an ethically nuanced wonder when we are placed before each living animal (2004a, 306; 2000b, chapter 2; 2004b, chapter 2). It is to be hoped that this wonder would inform the deliberations of future social contract theorists in the revised original position.

To sum up my view, three points should be made. First, Nussbaum is correct to separate two questions that Rawls conflates: who frames the principles of justice, and for whom are the principles of justice framed? Second, this separation makes it possible to consider the choice between the "trusteeship solution" to the problem of social contract theory and animals and the option that readily admits that social contract theory is insufficient to deal with animal entitlements. Nussbaum unfortunately thinks that the trusteeship solution (i.e., the revised original position) is not available to social contract theorists; hence she opts for the latter alternative. She, along with Rawls himself, thinks that the trusteeship solution is not available to social contract theorists because of the conditions that the framers of justice must be roughly equal in power and mental ability, on the one hand, and primarily or exclusively motivated by mutual advantage, on the other. I have tried to argue, however, that even the limited rough equality in question leaves open wide enough differences that there may well be species overlap between the least advantaged human beings and many animals. I have also tried to argue that Rawlsian *reasonableness,* in partial contrast to Rawlsian *rationality,* involves a willingness to enter the original position so as to seek justice. That is, the participants in Rawls's original position are motivated by

more than mutual advantage: their very presence in this position indicates that they *want* to be just! And third, Nussbaum thinks that it is both
the social contract component and the Kantian component of Rawls's
thought (the latter being derived from the anthropocentric character of
the Judeo-Christian tradition of *imago Dei,* wherein only human beings
deserve direct moral respect) that cause his problems with animals (see
Nussbaum 2006, 136–38, 332–35, 338–39, 349–50, 356). I have argued,
to the contrary, that social contract theory need not be part of the
problem.

REFLECTIVE EQUILIBRIUM

Nussbaum herself admits the compatibility between Rawlsian social contract theory and the capabilities approach at the methodological level: she
subscribes to Rawls's method of reflective equilibrium. Therefore, my
efforts in this chapter to bring Rawlsian social contract theory and the
capabilities approach together in the case of animals should be seen
against this larger methodological background. We have seen in chapter
1 that Rawls traces this method back to Aristotle, or better, to Socrates.
First, we carefully examine all of the relevant intuitions we have and the
judgments we make, asking which are the most basic (an Aristotelian's
language) or which are the considered judgments (a Rawlsian's language). Second, we investigate different theories that claim to organize
these intuitions and judgments. Nothing is held to be fixed. The goal is to
seek consistency and fit between (1) intuitions/judgments and (2) theory,
when they are taken together as a whole.

It is crucial in this method that we be able to revise our considered
judgments, and even our intuitions, if such revision is required by a
powerful theory, as I have argued. It is also possible that we might revise,
or even reject, a theory in the face of considered judgments or intuitions.
Neither component is fixed in advance. Rawls's powerful theory of justice, with its familiar original position and veil of ignorance, has altered
the considered judgments, even the intuitions, of many philosophers and
hordes of students over the past several decades.

It is my hope that some small contribution to the theory of justice can
be made by the revised original position detailed above. As a result of
this revised original position, narrative fiction (as Nussbaum emphasizes), and closer attention to our common sympathetic intuition in the

face of animal suffering, the human imagination can cross the species barrier. It is to be emphasized that Rawls himself notes that parties in the original position do not "bargain" in Hobbesian (strictly selfish) fashion, as Nussbaum sometimes implies. Rather, they deliberate, from the Latin *deliberare:* to weigh in mind, to ponder, to consider thoroughly (see Nussbaum 2006, 62, 174).

One way to classify the possible positions is to say that Scanlon and Rawls are social contract theorists who adopt a "descriptive" or conservative stance regarding animals, whereas I take a "deliberative" or revisionary stance, to use Scanlon's own terms (Scanlon 1998). Nussbaum's judicious use of reflective equilibrium seems to lie between these two positions. As I see things, however, the revised original position *should* put our considered (speciesist) judgments regarding animals into a troubling disequilibrium. Likewise, religious believers who subscribe to an omnibenevolent God who cares about even the fall of a sparrow (Matt. 10:29), and who also subscribe to the principle of *imitatio Dei,* would be remiss if they did not take seriously the arguments from sentiency and marginal cases.

4

A RAWLSIAN CRITIQUE OF LEGACY
AND AFFIRMATIVE ACTION

In 1999 it came to light that the person who was to become president of the United States was a "C" student and had undistinguished scores on standardized tests (Mayer and Robbins 1999). How then did George W. Bush get admitted to Yale and then to Harvard? The answer apparently has to do with certain "legacy" considerations, namely, the consideration that his wealthy and influential relatives were alumni of these prestigious institutions. Likewise, in the 2008 presidential election it came to light that John McCain had graduated in the bottom 1 percent of his class at the Naval Academy. Why, then, was he admitted in the first place? Once again, the answer seems to lie in the legacy created by his father and grandfather, both of whom graduated from this highly selective institution (Timberg 2007, 17–34).

The other major candidate, and eventual victor, in the 2008 American presidential election, Barack Obama, rightly accentuated his successful career at Harvard Law School. But Obama refused to make available, after repeated requests to do so, his Scholastic Aptitude Test (SAT) score and his grades while at Occidental College for two years. He likewise refused to release his Law School Admission Test (LSAT) score and his grades while at Columbia for two years (it is known, however, that he did not graduate from Columbia with honors). Although there can be no certainty here (Obama could eliminate all doubt by releasing the relevant data), it seems safe to assume that Obama's standardized test scores and grades at Occidental and Columbia were undistinctive. Obama himself admits that at this stage he was indifferent to school and that drugs, including cocaine, were a significant part of his life (2004, 93–96). So how did he get admitted to Occidental and then to Columbia and then to Harvard? The safest guess seems to be: affirmative action. (Because Obama's father went to graduate school at Harvard, Obama's admission to that institution, if not to Occidental and Columbia, might have been due to legacy considerations.)

Discussion of legacy and affirmative action admissions/hires tends to be heated. "Conservatives" tend to defend legacy admissions/hires and "liberals" tend to defend affirmative action admissions/hires. Hence it is not surprising that legacy and affirmative action admissions/hires are widespread. But it seems to me that they are conceptually problematic.

The purpose of this chapter is to offer a Rawlsian critique of both legacy and affirmative action admissions/hires, although I will eventually argue that legacy is a worse injustice than affirmative action. It is odd that Rawls never in his published writings explicitly stated his views of legacy and affirmative action—odd because these topics, especially affirmative action, have been hotly debated for several decades. One possible explanation for his silence on these subjects is that Rawls was primarily interested in ideal justice, whereas affirmative action in particular involves compensation for injustices, which signals the presence of nonideal conditions. But Rawls opined on several nonideal cases: war, abortion, euthanasia, campaign finance reform, school prayer (see, e.g., Rawls 1996, liii), and so on. Why not legacy and affirmative action?

I do not know how to attempt to answer this question. Rather, the purpose of this chapter is to offer a Rawls*ian* argument against legacy and affirmative action. Although I will carefully cite texts from Rawls himself throughout the chapter, my view is not so much lifted from Rawls's writings as it is constructed loosely on the basis of Rawls's insights. That is, I take responsibility for the way in which the argument is constructed. I am not trying to slip in through the back door the thesis that the parts of Rawls's thought that I have put together would have been put together by Rawls himself in order to make the cases against legacy and affirmative action. Once again, I am defending not Rawls's own view but a Rawls*ian* view.

Along with many other philosophers, I have the sense that, despite the enormous amount of attention that has been paid to Rawls's work, there is still more there that is worthy of analysis. I will admittedly be trying to sort out the interpretive diversity of opinion about Rawls and the twin phenomena of legacy and affirmative action. To cite just a few examples, Nicholas Wolterstorff thinks that "affirmative action is quite clearly incompatible with the concept of liberal democracy; it is, on the contrary, a strategy for undoing some of the consequences of our society's *not* having been a liberal democracy with respect to its treatment of women and people of color" (Wolterstorff and Audi 1997, 149; Wolterstorff 2008). By contrast, Anita Allen (2004) believes optimistically that a Rawlsian case for affirmative action could be made. Thomas Nagel seems to defend a view between these two extremes in holding that affirmative action is "not seriously unjust" (1979, 91; cf. 2003b, 72), which seems in some fashion to admit that it *is* unjust. Although my interpretation of Rawls on these issues is closest to that of Wolterstorff, I am much more favorably disposed toward Rawlsian political liberalism than Wolterstorff is.

As I mentioned in the preface, this chapter is less concerned with issues of religion than the other chapters are. But this admission should not be exaggerated. Defenders of legacy are the remote inheritors of the divine right of aristocracy and noblesse oblige, which Rawls himself explicitly rejects (see 1999c, 64, 100). And defenders of affirmative action often equate the quasi-religious (and understandable) battle against racism (which, for example, the abolitionists and Martin Luther King often base on a religious comprehensive doctrine) with (questionable) practices involved in affirmative action.

TAYLOR'S THESIS

Until recently the status of scholarship on Rawlsian affirmative action was inconclusive. As a result of Robert Taylor's magisterial article on the subject (2009), however, I think that we have a much clearer view of the relevant issues and challenges. As mentioned above, Rawls never explicitly addressed legacy or affirmative action in his writings, although some see an indirect reference to affirmative action in *Justice as Fairness* (2001, 65–66). We also have apocryphal evidence from some of Rawls's students that in conversation he may have permitted affirmative action, but

only for a limited time in nonideal theory because there is no place whatsoever for it in ideal theory, as Taylor notes. I will return to this distinction between ideal and nonideal theory in due course. Despite the paucity
of evidence in Rawls's own writings, Rawls*ian* arguments have been constructed both for (e.g., Nagel 2003a) and against (e.g., Sher 1979) affirmative action. The present chapter is intended largely to support the
latter cause. The case I will make depends on the idea that Rawlsian
deontological ideal theory is meant to constrain nonideal theory, as Rawls
himself argues.

In order to indicate how my account adds something significant to
Taylor's, however, I must briefly distinguish the five sorts of affirmative
action that Taylor treats: (1) There is equality of opportunity or, as Rawls
refers to it, careers open to talents. (2) There is "aggressive" equality
of opportunity, as in sensitivity training for employers and admissions
committees. (3) Minority applicants are offered support, as in financial
backing. (4) There are soft quota programs, as in giving bonus points to
members of targeted groups. And (5) there are hard quotas, as in job
or college representation for targeted groups that is proportional to the
percentage of the targeted group in the general population.

Taylor's carefully defended thesis is that in justice as fairness, considered as ideal theory, only (1) and (2) are required, while (3), (4), and (5)
are prohibited. Here I agree with Taylor, as long as two qualifications are
made. The first is that, in terms of Wittgensteinian meaning as use, in
American popular culture (1) is not normally called a type of affirmative
action. Indeed, it is often spoken of in opposition to affirmative action.
The second qualification is that (2) is *permissible* within justice as fairness
as long as it does not degenerate into an offensive sort of paternalism.
As I see things, only (1) is actually *required* by justice as fairness. Taylor
seems to agree, as when he suggests that (2) is easier to justify under
nonideal theory than under ideal theory.

A corollary of Taylor's thesis is that under nonideal theory (3) would
also be permissible. That is, (4) and (5) are ruled out within justice as
fairness even under nonideal theory. I agree with Taylor in his opposition
to (4) and (5), but it seems to me that (3) violates fair equality of opportunity, as I will explain.

In any event, Taylor is helpful in clarifying the difference between two
different components of fair equality of opportunity: formal equality of
opportunity and substantive equality of opportunity. (I prefer to call the
latter material equality of opportunity in that formal equality is hardly

insubstantial.) The latter concerns the structure of society and its ability to enable citizens to take real advantage of fair equality of opportunity. Someone living in grinding poverty might not be in a position to value and/or take advantage of fair equality of opportunity, as Marxists have traditionally argued. Fair enough. I will argue, however, that the legitimate claims that can be made in favor of material equality of opportunity do not constitute a case for the suspension of formal equality of opportunity. In fact, formal equality of opportunity is lexically prior to material equality of opportunity in justice as fairness.

It should be noted that there seem to be two ways in which to determine the realm of nonideal theory: some actions (e.g., war) are simply in a different *category* from ideal theory, on the one hand, whereas some actions are *exceptions to an ideal rule,* on the other (see Rawls 1999c, 8; 2001, 13). The goal of both types of nonideal theory, however, ought to be to figure out how, in less than ideal conditions, to create the conditions wherein ideal theory could more readily apply (Korsgaard 1996). So if ideal theory is relaxed, what is acceptable in nonideal theory should not be determined by utilitarian criteria, whether explicitly or implicitly. Rather, the court of appeal should judge in terms of justice as fairness as construed in ideal theory, especially in terms of the principles of justice lexically ordered. Here Taylor distinguishes, along with Tamar Schapiro, between the letter of ideal theory and its spirit. He makes this distinction in order to permit some types of affirmative action that violate the letter of lexical ordering but that (supposedly) are consistent with its spirit.

I am skeptical as to whether this distinction does the intellectual work that Taylor wants it to do, but I understand his point. One way to make the distinction between ideal and nonideal theory, he thinks, is to say that in the former both the letter and spirit of the principles of justice and their lexical ordering are necessary conditions, whereas in the latter only the spirit of justice is required. The question is whether the "fudging" of lexically ordered principles permitted in nonideal theory constitutes an abandonment of the very deontological constraints (e.g., the distinctness of persons) that make justice as fairness the unique position that it is and that enable it to offer such a powerful critique of utilitarianism. For example, even in nonideal theory it is better to equalize funding of elementary education than to try to determine later exactly which applicants received lower scores on standardized tests because of lower funding levels at their elementary schools, and exactly which students received lower scores due to other factors, determinations that are obviously impossible.

Although Taylor is more willing than I am to walk down the road of nonideal theory (i.e., he is a bit more comfortable than I am with [2] and [3]), he is well aware of the potholes he is likely to hit. Suppose the conditions of fair equality of opportunity could more readily be achieved by publicly executing those convicted of racial or gender discrimination. Defenders of (3), (4), and (5) would no doubt reject this option, but why? Or again, suppose that the fastest way to bring about fair equality of opportunity is to have a nationwide policy prohibiting the hiring or admitting of white males (even from poor or lower-middle-class backgrounds) until racial and gender parity has been achieved. As in the case of public execution, this policy might really "work." It is understandable, I think, why some might easily conclude after considering these cases that the driving force at work here is utilitarian rather than deontological.

It might be asked, what exactly does it mean to say that we can violate the letter if not the spirit of fair equality of opportunity? Certainly not that we could kill applicants who are not in the targeted group. But can we lie to them (quite ironically, white lies)? Or treat their applications unfairly? These questions are not merely hypothetical.

It is to Taylor's credit that he notices that the mere fact that a group is underrepresented in a specific occupation or institution is no more at odds with justice than is the fact that some groups are statistically overrepresented. For example, that almost 40 percent of Nobel laureates in economics have been Jewish does not in itself prove that Jews have had an unfair advantage in that field (see Taylor 2009, nn56–57). It is also to Taylor's credit that he rejects, on a Rawlsian basis, the more muscular versions of affirmative action, that is, (4) and (5). But it is precisely these types of affirmative action that are normally intended when people speak in favor of affirmative action. Varieties (4) and (5) of affirmative action violate both the spirit and the letter of fair equality of opportunity, assuming for the moment the cogency of this distinction. To pursue these, Taylor argues, is to try to bring about a just society through unjust means. This is in contrast to the goal of fair competitive conditions; and these conditions cannot be secured simultaneously while guaranteeing certain outcomes.

It would be a mistake, however, to assume that these fair competitive conditions are part of a meritocracy. There are at least two reasons why one should avoid describing justice as fairness as a meritocracy in its opposition to legacy and affirmative action. First, fair equality of opportunity is integrally connected to our higher-order interest in self-realization through work, as Taylor insightfully points out, and this connection is more important than whatever we might gain by way of monetary rewards or societal honors; and second, it is also integrally connected to all of the goods—primary or otherwise—to which we are entitled even if we have done nothing to earn or merit them. By considering these two reasons together we can better understand why it is true that in a just society even those who were not admitted to medical school or who were not awarded a promotion in the fire department would still be able to pursue their higher-order interests, given their talents according to the Aristotelian principle. That is, they would not be left out in the cold, as they might be in a libertarian version of meritocracy.

In justice as fairness all citizens would receive the social basis for self-respect, they would have equal fundamental liberties with other citizens, and they would have the material support to make these liberties meaningful. What they would not have is the (legacy or affirmative action) right to be admitted to medical school over someone with higher test scores or to be promoted within the fire department over someone who (perhaps through great effort) scored significantly higher on the fire officer examination.

Thus far I have indicated agreement with Taylor on the necessity of (1) and regarding the impermissibility of (4) and (5). Further, I have expressed more skepticism than Taylor about (2) and (3), but even he is commendably tentative in his support of these two sorts of affirmative action.

In the remainder of this chapter I would like to state my own argument, which tries to supplement Taylor's landmark approach in two ways. First, at several points Taylor alludes to Rawls's lexically ordered principles of justice, but he does not lay out in a detailed way the reasons for these orderings (the plural is crucial here, as I will show). I think that it is important to do this because, as I see things, legacy and affirmative action are typically morally bothersome precisely because they violate the lexical ordering of the principles of justice. And second, I will tie my opposition to affirmative action to my opposition to legacy. I have been told that such a conjunction is silly, given the obvious differences between legacy and affirmative action. But to claim that there is an analogy between the two, rather than an identity relation, is already to admit that there are differences between legacy and affirmative action. The important thing to notice here, however, is that these two are similar in the way they violate ideal justice by way of arbitrariness. And, if I understand Taylor correctly, it is the signal achievement of liberalism generally to have eliminated, or to be on the way to eliminating, arbitrary advantages due to religion initially, but then eventually to advantages due to class, race, sex, sexual orientation, and so on.

THE CORE OF THE ARGUMENT

My argument proceeds by way of four steps. I will first lay out the core of my Rawlsian stance, and then I will lay out the implications of the core argument, as I see them, for legacy and affirmative action admissions/hires. One can detect a sort of chain connection, to use language from Rawls, between the highly publicized examples of legacy and affirmative action mentioned above from the stratospheric region of real power, to mid-range examples, all the way down to quotidian examples that are found in most universities and many workplaces. Legacy and affirmative action admissions/hires are still very much with us and, as I see things, provide obstacles to a closer approximation of a just society.

(a) *Justice has priority over efficiency.* That justice is the first virtue of social institutions, as truth is of systems of thought, is a matter of intuitive conviction. The implications of this priority are far reaching, as we will see. To say that justice is lexicographically prior to efficiency (in the Pareto sense) is to make use of a dictionary metaphor: a comes before b, and so on. The first principle in a lexicographical (or more simply, lexical or serial) order must be satisfied before we consider the second, the second before the third, and so forth. The whole point of having a serial ordering of principles is to facilitate reflective equilibrium by avoiding vague balancing of principles if at all possible. The earlier principles are more heavily weighted than the later ones. Of course, there are no obvious rules when equally weighted principles themselves conflict, but regarding the present priority, at least, it is easier to achieve reflective equilibrium if we stick with our intuition that justice has priority over efficiency (and that moral considerations trump nonmoral ones). That is, rejecting this priority would throw almost everything else in theory of justice into disequilibrium. For example, if we rejected this priority, then efficient forms of serfdom or slavery would be morally permissible

(Rawls 1999c, 3–4, 37–40, 61, 69, 264, 298–99; 1999a, 348; Freeman 2007a, 63–66).

(b) *The first principle of justice is prior to the second.* The first principle of justice, that each person is to have an equal right to the most extensive total system of equal basic liberties compatible with a similar system of liberty for all, is famous. Almost as famous is its priority to the second principle. The justification here is not solely by way of appeal to an intuition that, if rejected, would put theory of justice into disequilibrium. Nor is this priority self-evident. Rather, its principal justification is by way of appeal to the original position. That is, the priority of the first principle to the second principle is what would be chosen as a fair term of agreement (Rawls 1999c, 37–39).

Rawls treats the priority in question at length in four sections of *A Theory of Justice* (8, 39, 46, 82), indicating that it is integral to any Rawlsian approach. The key idea is that teleological theories, in contrast to deontological ones, provide uncertain grounds for equal liberty. If a basic liberty is regulated or restricted, this should be done only for the sake of liberty itself, as when the lesser liberty of children is justified in terms of both the child's *natural* limitation at present and the eventual amelioration of this limitation as the child grows into an adult with equal liberty. Or again, there may be *social* limitations that will require that we regulate or restrict liberty for the sake of liberty. For example, reasonable discourse will not flourish if everyone speaks at once, hence the need to regulate, if not restrict, free speech. And the liberty of the intolerant may at times need to be controlled for the sake of liberty itself. In any event, it is the deliberation that occurs in the original position that would justify such regulation or restriction. The common hope is that the restriction of liberty would eventually no longer be needed. Hence, although this priority is not intuitive or self-evident, it is part of the considered convictions of democratic peoples (Rawls 1999c, 131–32, 213–20; 2001, 111).

What is ruled out is the exchange of a supposed lesser liberty for greater social or economic advantages. The reciprocity and equality among persons in the original position is seen by its participants to be worthy of preservation, hence the priority of the first principle. By securing the higher-order interests enshrined in the first principle, a certain sort of regulative ideal is established that reasonable-rational deliberators would refuse to abandon. As Rawls puts the point (with the first sentence having particular import regarding legacy, but in a secondary way regarding affirmative action as well): "Thus when the belief in a fixed natural order sanctioning a hierarchical society is abandoned, assuming here that this belief is not true, a tendency is set up in the direction of the two principles of justice in serial order. The effective protection of the equal liberties becomes increasingly of first importance in support of self-respect and this affirms the precedence of the first principle" (1999c, 480, also 474–76). Rawls is quite clear that the fact that this priority would be chosen in the original position provides more justification than would appear at first sight. It places the burden of proof squarely on the shoulders of the person who wants to regulate or restrict liberty for some reason other than liberty itself. And it should be emphasized that the liberties at stake here are not those that are dear to laissez-faire capitalists, like the freedom to own the means of production (Rawls 1999c, 53–55), in that, despite the priority of the first principle, the two principles of justice hang together organically as part of a single theory of justice.

The basic liberties are inalienable in the sense that they cannot be waived or overridden by collective social or economic preferences but only by liberty itself. Because the basic liberties are not on the same plane as these other considerations, and this because they are the result of a fair selection process, they serve to secure the ties of social unity rather than work against them. Citizens affirm that there are different irreconcilable, yet reasonable, conceptions of the good. But the priority of the first principle nonetheless enables people to affirm a shared sense of justice despite the different comprehensive doctrines that citizens affirm. Natural liberty is thereby enhanced by a contract that reasonable/rational agents willingly endorse (Rawls 1999a, 161, 260, 348, 362, 372, 385).

This enhancement in part consists in providing, via the priority of the first principle, the necessary condition for other needs and interests to be met. In different terms, the second principle, of which the difference principle is a part, presupposes background institutions that satisfy the priority of the first principle and thus prevent "trade-offs" between basic rights, on the one hand, and social or economic benefits, on the other. Of course, no basic liberty is absolute in that it can be alienated for the sake of liberty itself. It is the whole scheme of equal liberties that has priority (Rawls 2001, 44–47, 104–5, 111).

The basic liberties covered by the first principle enable us to become free and equal citizens in the first place. To sum up, in a just society, "Citizens do not think there are antecedent social ends that justify them in viewing some people as having more or less worth to society than others and assigning them different basic rights and privileges accordingly. Many past societies have thought otherwise: they pursued as final ends religion and empire, dominion and glory; and the rights and status of individuals and classes have depended on their role in gaining those ends" (Rawls 1996, 41, also 6, 312–24).

(c) *Within the second principle of justice, the equality of opportunity principle is prior to the difference principle.* The reason for this priority is closely allied to the argument found in step (b) above. Equal opportunity has an amphibious character: it swims in the sea of social and economic benefit and, as a result, is lexically subsequent to the first principle. Equal opportunity is always equal opportunity to something or other, like admission to college or a job hire. In another sense, however, equal opportunity can be seen as conceptually allied to the basic liberties that are given priority in the first principle. That is, one's *rights* are violated if one is not treated fairly in an educational admission or job hire process. In this sense, equal opportunity walks on the secure soil of the first principle and its protection of basic liberties. Because of this amphibious status, it has priority over the difference principle, which is centered on social and economic benefit and hence is lexically subsequent to the first principle, which is centered on basic freedoms when seen in abstraction from social and economic benefit. As I see things, this "in-between" status captures well the place of equal opportunity in a just society (Rawls 1999c, sections 14, 46; 1999a, 362, 392; 2001, 43).

Equality of opportunity means the idea that social and economic inequalities are to be arranged so that they are attached to offices and positions open to all under fair conditions; further, as we have seen, equality of opportunity for all is integrally connected to our higher-order interest in self-realization through work. The reason why these conditions should be fair for everyone has to do not with efficiency considerations but with justice considerations, as detailed above in steps (a) and (b). It is not fair to have one's realization of self debarred by unjust admission or hiring practices. To make the point subjectively, one's expectation that one will be treated fairly in an application or hiring practice is "legitimate" (Rawls 1999c, 74). Rawls himself cites as unjust Burke's and Hegel's defenses of the prerogatives of great families and the legitimacy of primogeniture. That society benefits from primogeniture (if in fact it does) is not relevant from the standpoint of the original position (264).

It might seem that in nonideal circumstances inequality of opportunity can occur if it enhances the opportunities of those with the lesser opportunity (Rawls 1999c, 266), but Rawls himself is clear in a very important passage that "the ranking of the principles of justice in ideal theory reflects back and guides the application of these principles to non-ideal situations" (267). The goal should be the good of equal opportunity, not the evil of inequality of opportunity, which, if it should be tolerated at all, should be permitted only reluctantly and temporarily. Presumably this is close to what Nagel was getting at, as mentioned above. There is an analogy to the evil of slavery here, which could perhaps be tolerated reluctantly and temporarily in a nonideal, in extremis case where the only alternative was that those to be enslaved were to be tortured and killed instead. Even in nonideal circumstances we should be guided by the priority rules, including the priority of the equality of opportunity principle to the difference principle (131, 218).

It should be emphasized again that positions should be open not only in a formal sense, in that all should have a real chance to attain them. Rawls admits that this view might sound vague, but the forceful language he uses in his attempt to clarify matters should not escape our notice: "those with similar abilities and skills should have similar life chances," and "those who are at the same level of talent and ability, and have the same willingness to use them, should have the same prospects of success regardless of their initial place in the social system" (1999c, 63; also 1999a, 161). This insistence that equal opportunity not be purely formal is meant to distinguish justice as fairness from a laissez-faire type of natural liberty wherein "careers open to talents" are not held in check by the principles (including the difference principle) that would be agreed to in a fair decision-making procedure. The difference principle, the idea that social and economic inequalities are to be arranged so that they can reasonably be expected to promote everyone's advantage (especially the least advantaged), does operate in a crucial way in a just society, but only against the background of "equality of opportunity and a fair competition for the available positions on the basis of reasonable qualifications" (1999a, 138).

(d) *Within the equality of opportunity principle, formal (or negative) equality of opportunity is prior to material (or positive) equality of opportunity.* Here, more than in the previous three steps, my view relies on interpretive industry, but I nonetheless think that this priority is both defensible and does justice to Rawls's best insights. In fact, I allege that by defending this priority a genuine advance can be made in the understanding of a Rawlsian view of legacy and affirmative action. The key idea here is the commonplace in ethical theory that one's first duty is to do no harm. That is, negative duties have a certain priority over positive duties. In analogous fashion, perfect duties have a certain priority over imperfect duties. By making these claims, however, one is not committed to the denigration of, much less the elimination of, positive or imperfect duties.

Consider Rawls's treatment of natural duties, those that apply to us without regard to our voluntary acts and have no necessary connection to institutions or social practices. In most cases the distinction between negative natural duties and positive natural duties is intuitively clear. In such cases "negative duties have more weight than positive ones" (1999c, 98). As examples of the former, Rawls cites the duties not to be cruel, not to injure another, and not to cause unnecessary suffering. As an example of the latter he cites the duty to help another. The intuitive ideas here are that a promise not to be cruel would be redundant, hence the appropriateness of the adjective "natural," and that opposition to the priority of negative duties would throw almost everything else we believe in ethics into disequilibrium (cf. Nussbaum 2006, 372–73). For example, it is hard to see how we could praise a torturer or a murderer who nonetheless gave a great deal of money to a soup kitchen. Less histrionic examples could be given. Although I think that the duty to help others *is* a duty, the fact that this positive duty to help others is often seen, by both philosophers and citizens in popular culture, as supererogatory rather than as a duty is further evidence in favor of the priority of negative duties (Rawls 1999c, 100, 293–301).

The first task here should be to eliminate arbitrary, and hence unfair, barriers to educational admissions and employment. The desire to positively help others secure admission or find employment, however, is not a trump card that can be played at the expense of others, regardless of whether this desire is based on commendable or envious motives (see Nagel 2003b, 66–69, 72, 77, 84). The primary goal is to make sure that differences among people are "handled by the social practices of qualifying for positions and free competition against the background of fair equality of opportunity, including fair equality of opportunity in education, together with the regulation of inequalities in income and wealth by the difference principle" (Rawls 1996, 184). The priorities defended in (a), (b), and (c) above have an effect on the priority found here in (d): the regulation of social and economic advantages can occur in a fair manner only against a background where no one's rights are overridden (228).

Rawls goes out of his way to defend the practice of making sure that advertisements for jobs and educational opportunities reach everyone in the population, especially those who might be qualified and who previously would have been denied fair equality of opportunity. But the goal is, in fact, that "social and economic inequalities are to be attached to offices and positions open to everyone under conditions of fair equality of opportunity" (1996, 363). That is, the advertisements must be "consistent with the other requirements of justice" (364).

Because the two principles of justice work in tandem, the prior principles do have distributive effects. On the one hand, the difference principle cannot be taken seriously all by itself apart from the prior principles (Rawls 1996, 46). On the other hand, strict adherence to the prior principles, including the priority of formal (or negative) equal opportunity to material (or positive) equal opportunity, leads to a more egalitarian distribution of social and economic goods than has ever existed historically, even in the social welfare states (Daniels 2003). Indeed, such an adherence leads to just distribution. This is in clear contrast to the political and economic inequalities possessed historically on the basis of religion or race or sex, which were clearly not to the advantage of everyone in society, especially the least advantaged (Rawls 2001, 64–66).

The sort of equality of opportunity that is defensible is that which occurs in an "open system," a system that "assures equally good education and chances of culture for all and which keeps open the competition for positions on the basis of qualities reasonably related to performance" (Rawls 1999a, 143, 159). Contrary to what many people mistakenly think, Rawls is not describing a welfare state, with its exaggerated sense of positive duty, a state that nonetheless deprives the least advantaged of the basic good of the social basis of self-respect. The social basis of self-respect is a crucial good, as any careful reader of Rawls realizes. What is not often considered is that legacy and affirmative action frequently corrode this good, as we see when recipients of legacy and affirmative action become defensive when the details of their admission/hire are brought to their attention. By contrast, Rawls is describing here a type of property-owning democracy (1999a, 419–20; 2001, part 4; see also Appiah 2002; and Mandle 2009 on property-owning democracy).

Likewise, our first duty internationally involves the effort to avoid an exaggerated sense of positive duty. Our first duty is to refrain from invading other societies, from exploiting them, and so on. The positive obligation of assistance is subsequent to these negative duties and applies, for the most part, to our relations with "burdened societies"—for example, those where people are dying of starvation-related diseases (Rawls 1999a, 559; 1999b, part 3).

No doubt the Marxist objection will be raised that the sort of justice I am defending in this chapter secures only the formal (or negative) liberties (e.g., freedom *from* obstruction by others). The proper Rawlsian response should be that in a just property-owning democracy, the joint operation of the fair equality of opportunity principle and the difference principle gives adequate protection to positive liberties (e.g., the freedom *to* make choices conducive to self-realization). Once again, the two principles of justice, when seen as functioning together, albeit in serial order, should allay the fear that liberal freedoms are purely formal or purely negative. Indeed, what it means to defend *fair* equality of opportunity is to ensure that such equality not be merely formal (Rawls 2007, 321).

Before leaving the priority of formal equality of opportunity to material equality of opportunity, I would like to situate this priority within what I have called the amphibious character of equality of opportunity in general. Recall that equality of opportunity is conceptually allied with both the basic liberties (in that one's rights are violated if one is not treated fairly in an educational admissions or a job hire process; thus one can legitimately expect that one will be treated fairly in these contexts) and with economic benefit (in that equal opportunity is always equal opportunity to some good result or other). Because of the priority of the first principle of justice to the second, that part of equal opportunity that is connected to the first principle of justice has priority to that part of equal opportunity that is connected to the difference principle. That is, my view here regarding (d) relies on the claims made above regarding (b). To reject the priority of formal equality of opportunity to material equality of opportunity is to put into disequilibrium the priority of liberty in general.

IMPLICATIONS OF THE ARGUMENT

If the priorities discussed above are ordered correctly, I claim, it becomes very difficult to defend legacy or affirmative action admissions/hires. Further, despite some obvious differences between legacy and affirmative action, the two are not, as is often assumed, radically different. That is, they both run afoul of the priorities discussed above and often for the same reasons.

Concerning priority (a), from the time of book 1 of Plato's *Republic,* it has been customary to start discussions of justice by initially defining the term as rendering to *each* his or her due. Although this preliminary definition does not tell us precisely what each is due, it nonetheless does notable intellectual work. If justice is the first virtue of social institutions, such that it is prior to other features of social institutions like efficiency, then we should be wary of waving away injustices, as Nagel does, because they are supposedly not serious.

Not serious to whom? To a student who had higher high school grades and higher SAT scores than George W. Bush but who was denied admission to Yale the same year that Bush was accepted on a legacy basis, the injustice involved might very well be serious. Indeed, it might lead the student to become cynical about American society, especially if those in power turn a deaf ear to his or her protests.

Or again, it is often assumed (incorrectly, I think) that affirmative action admissions like Barack Obama are not problematic because a student not admitted to Occidental or Columbia or Harvard, despite having higher grades and higher scores on standardized tests than Obama, could easily land on his or her feet elsewhere. But this is to assume that the denied student came from an advantaged background. That is, it is to assume that the student has an untapped legacy at his or her disposal. To be frank, to those more highly qualified lower-middle-class or poor students or job applicants, who are neither winners in the social lottery nor positioned to become beneficiaries of affirmative action, both legacy and affirmative action *are* serious injustices. These people do not receive their due. That is, they do not benefit from what Rawls assumes will be "chain connection" among the different economic classes in society (1999c, 70–73).

Further, priority (b) alerts us to the unjust, yet frequent, trade-offs that occur between the infringement of the right to have one's application considered fairly, on the one hand, and alleged social benefit, on the other. To update a famous example from a generation ago, once Allan Bakke graduated from medical school, he practiced medicine in rural Minnesota, which is almost exclusively white. Hence greater social benefit would have occurred, it is suggested, if a minority applicant to Cal-Davis's medical school had been accepted in Bakke's place, because that applicant would have been more likely to serve populations historically underserved by the medical profession (see Ball 2000).

Three comments are in order here. First, even on a utilitarian basis it is by no means obvious that the case against Bakke's admission is defensible. After all, rural communities have also been historically underserved by the medical profession.

But second, my argument is not utilitarian. Rather, it follows familiar deontological objections to legacy and affirmative action. Applicants whose fathers and grandfathers did not attend the Naval Academy should not have been disadvantaged when they competed against John McCain for admission. And Bakke, who had better grades and a higher Medical College Admission Test (MCAT) score than minority applicants who were admitted, but who was twice denied admission to medical school before the Supreme Court made it possible for him to be admitted, was initially treated unfairly. Rawls's original position argument that teleological theories in general provide uncertain grounds for equal liberty is yet to be refuted. *Even if* greater social and economic benefit would be gained by lesser liberty, which is questionable, it is by no means clear that it would be rational to restrict liberty for some reason other than liberty itself. In extremis conditions sometimes force us to alienate liberty for the sake of liberty itself, but in a fair decision-making procedure basic liberties remain inalienable vis-à-vis social and economic benefit.

And third, it is not often noticed that the most sophisticated sort of justification for legacy admissions/hires is very similar in important respects to teleological arguments used in defense of affirmative action. (I am assuming that natural hierarchy arguments based on divine right are, thankfully, not too persuasive these days, as Rawls implies in his treatment of Rousseau [2007, 246].) For example, E. Digby Baltzell, the prominent sociologist who coined the acronym "WASP," thought that legacy was a good thing in that society tends to fall apart, or at least to wallow in mediocrity, without the leadership provided by talented, civilized, aristocratic families. That is, the lesser liberty of those who compete against the Bushes and the McCains is outweighed, on a Baltzellian line of reasoning, by the betterment of society these families bring about. This is a dangerous argument, in my view. Not only does it entail nepotism (literally, nephew-ism), which in my experience leads to incompetent people being admitted/hired, but by accepting it we would also place many considered beliefs of reflective people in liberal democracies into disequilibrium. Thus the ties of social unity are secured, rather than severed, by opposition to legacy admissions/hires. Likewise, I claim, regarding opposition to affirmative action.

Or again, legacies are sometimes defended because of their fund-raising potential for private universities, a potential that, if actualized, helps both to sustain private universities in general and to cross-subsidize deserving poor or lower-middle-class students in particular. My response to this argument is the same as that found in the previous paragraph, in that such legacies violate priorities (a) and (b). One could even go so far as to call legacy and affirmative action types of "tyranny," in Walzer's sense of the term (1983, 18–19, 143–54).

Priority (c) forces us to focus on the crucial concept of equal opportunity, which Seana Valentine Shiffrin rightly says critics have underemphasized (2004; cf. Alexander 1985; Arneson 1999). But to pay needed attention to the concept does not necessarily help the case for affirmative action. Shiffrin rightly resists the reduction of equal opportunity to the difference principle, with its sea of social and economic benefit. But this does not necessarily mean that it should be elevated completely to the secure status of the first principle. Rather, as I have characterized it, equal opportunity has an "amphibious" status. In some sense it *is* related to social and economic benefit, in that equal opportunity has to be opportunity to get something or other, like college admission or a job.

The key point is that inequality of opportunity would not be agreed to in the original position, not even if the justification would be the generation of wealth and status in nonideal circumstances. I take it that Rawls's point here is crucial in the effort to find a defensible theory of justice: ideal theory is not jettisoned in nonideal circumstances. Rather, it *guides* us when we find ourselves in nonideal circumstances. That is the whole point to having a theory of justice! I realize that I am open to the charge of hyperbole when I compare the toleration of inequality of opportunity with the toleration of slavery. I admit that the latter is far worse than the former. But the analogy holds, I think: inequality of opportunity is an evil that should be tolerated only under in extremis conditions, and even then it is important to acknowledge that it *is* an evil.

Rawls is correct, I think, to use phrases like "fair competition," "qualifying for positions," "those with similar abilities and skills," "those who are at the same level of talent and ability," and those who "have the same willingness to use them." He is focusing on the relevant, as opposed to irrelevant (hence arbitrary and unfair) criteria, which defenders of legacy and affirmative action fail to do.

In response to the charge that I have failed to adequately separate legacy and affirmative action, I would like to say forthrightly that I consider legacy a worse injustice than affirmative action. Intuitively it seems worse for those who are socially advantaged to benefit from inequality of opportunity than for those who historically have been socially disadvantaged to do so. But this does not make affirmative action just, for it, too, is a type of inequality of opportunity that is not justified by the production of greater social or economic benefit. It should be noted that although Rawls never explicitly condemns either legacy or affirmative action, he comes very close to condemning legacy when he criticizes the prerogatives of great families and primogeniture. Perhaps this suggests that he, too, finds legacy more unjust than affirmative action.

I should also note that legacy is a worse injustice than affirmative action because of its *aims*. At best, the defenders of legacy aim at financial rewards for an educational institution, say, and at worst they aim at perpetuating (an indefensible) hierarchy. By contrast, the defenders of affirmative action have the noble aim of trying to find an appropriate response to historical injustice. But in my view affirmative action is not a defensible way to achieve this aim.

Regarding priority (d) I would emphasize that the duty not to gain an unfair advantage over others is a formal (or negative) duty, and that I think it would be a significant event in the history of ethics if priority (d) were overturned. In Rawlsian language, rejecting priority (d) would put many other considered beliefs held by morally sensitive people in liberal democracies into disequilibrium. That is, rejecting (d) is too great a price to pay. The duty not to be cruel is *really* basic, I think. Although the duty not to gain unfair advantage over others is not quite so basic as the duty not to be cruel, it nonetheless has priority over the duty to positively or materially help others secure admission to college or find a job. Given the organic wholeness of the two principles of Rawlsian justice, we need not fear when Rawls speaks of "free competition" for socially desirable positions.

Although Anita Allen commends Robert Allen for developing a Rawlsian approach to affirmative action, such a commendation makes sense only if different senses of affirmative action are taken into account (A. Allen 2004; R. Allen 2004), as we have seen above with respect to Taylor's view. For example, if affirmative action means that we should advertise widely for educational and job opportunities, such that those advertisements reach those who previously would have been denied fair equality of opportunity, then along with Rawls I would agree that affirmative action is defensible, even desirable, in that it could be agreed to as a fair term of agreement. But the term "affirmative action" at present usually means something quite different. As Robert Allen notes, many victims of affirmative action in this latter sense have received significant harm if diversity is purchased at the cost of violating rights (see also Pojman 1992). Affirmative action as a recruitment tool does not necessarily violate rights. But affirmative action that contradicts concern for talents, abilities, skills, and the willingness to use them (to use Rawls's own language), as well as fair competition and qualifying for positions, *does* violate rights.

Although Rawls is often (and legitimately) seen as an opponent of meritocracy, this does not necessarily mean that there is no place whatsoever for merit in a just society. As Rawls puts it, "any offices having special benefits must be won in a fair competition in which contestants are judged on their *merits*" (1999a, 76, emphasis added). In sum, only those versions of legacy and affirmative action are legitimate that are consistent with the requirements of justice as detailed in priorities (a) through (d).

DISTRIBUTIVE JUSTICE

Whereas defenders of legacy and affirmative action say that we need these practices in order to preserve the free and equal status of citizens, I am arguing that without the aforementioned priorities there would be no free and equal citizens in the first place. But however strong or weak my argument has been thus far, I acknowledge that something else is needed, some indication of what I am for in addition to what I am against. Further, I would like to distance myself as far as possible from those opponents of affirmative action who were, or would have been, opponents as well of the Civil Rights Act of 1964 (e.g., Ronald Reagan). That is, I oppose legacy and affirmative action not despite my Rawlsian political liberalism but because of it.

Participants in the original position would not know their religion or their family background or their race or their sex (e.g., Rawls 1999c, 129; 1996, 24–25; 2001, 15). This ignorance makes it very unlikely that they would agree to legacy or affirmative action. But what they *would* agree to are the two principles of justice as working in tandem, albeit in serial order, resulting in a just distribution of wealth and other social goods, as I have previously noted. Further, as a consequence of agreeing to the first principle, they would be opposed to religion-based, family-based, race-based, or sex-based discrimination (see Shelby 2004, 1697–1710).

But there are other implications of the decisions made in the original position and in the four-stage sequence that occurs afterward, as the veil of ignorance is partially lifted at each stage (Rawls 1999c, 171–76). The list is impressive: there would be energetic (but nonpaternalistic) measures to address discrimination in the workplace, universal health care, jobs for all who want to work, the elimination of private contributions to political candidates (the elimination of "the curse of money," as Rawls puts it), regulation if not elimination of inherited wealth, a decent distribution of wealth so that all citizens could make effective use of their basic freedoms, sufficient funding for schools in all neighborhoods, and so on (e.g., Rawls 1997, 772; 1999b, 50; 2001, 53, 173–74; also Shelby 2004, 1711). In this regard we should take seriously Martin Carcieri's claim that, from a Rawlsian point of view, the funding of better schools and health facilities for blacks fares better than affirmative action policies in part because the former diffuses the burden of race policy over the entire taxpaying public, whereas the latter is especially unfair in the way it concentrates the burden of race policy on a smaller number of citizens who are applicants for particular positions (Carcieri 2010; see also Mandle 2009, 27–28, 32–33, 89, 167).

We have seen that because of these measures a Rawlsian society would involve a more egalitarian distribution of social and economic goods than has ever existed historically (see Daniels 2003). As Tommy Shelby puts this remarkable point, these measures "might . . . [even] have the effect of sharply reducing the resentment for past racial injustice that some members of disadvantaged racial groups harbor" (2004, 1712; cf. Graham 2010, 65–67, who thinks that Shelby's debt to Rawls is at odds with his commitment to a culture free of white supremacy). But these measures would no doubt anger those who had previously benefited from legacy admissions and hires. As before, legacy is a worse injustice than affirmative action.

Because legacy and affirmative action are huge topics, I have not alleged in this chapter that I have exhaustively examined all of the relevant issues in general, or even all of the relevant philosophical issues in particular. But I have arranged in lexical order what I take to be four defensible Rawlsian principles, and I claim to have done so is such a way as to clearly indicate what is morally problematic in legacy and affirmative action admissions/hires. Of course, any one, or all, of these four priorities could be rejected. The question is: would such a rejection lead us closer to a just society, or would it push into disequilibrium many of the beliefs held by those who take seriously the deliberations that occur in the Rawlsian original position?

My suspicion is that those who are skeptical of the Rawlsian approach I have defended in this chapter tend erroneously to associate Rawls's view of distributive justice with the "trickle-down" approach of laissez-faire capitalism, wherein the least advantaged are an afterthought, rather than with his own "suffuse upwards" approach of property-owning democracy, wherein the least advantaged are at the forefront of any effort to deviate from equality. One should remain acutely aware of the material impediments to equality of opportunity posed by inadequate educational institutions and excessive accumulation of wealth.

But Freeman informs us that Rawls himself did not see these impediments as justifying affirmative action programs as long-term solutions to the problem of injustice. Such solutions are more likely to be found in securing the social basis for self-respect in all citizens via approximation to justice (see Freeman 2007b, xii, 65, 90–91, 94, 99, 452). Or again, neither legacy nor affirmative action is defensible in ideal theory. And legacy is indefensible in nonideal theory as well. But from these conclusions we should not further conclude that affirmative action is defensible in nonideal theory as a long-term solution to the problems that it is meant to correct (see Freeman 2007a, 117, 262, 312).

Granted, even if there are no legal restrictions on entry into favorable positions, there could be an injustice done if such positions were determined largely by social connections and class bias. This is precisely the injustice involved in legacy hires/admissions, an injustice that I have explicitly identified as worse than that involved in affirmative action. That is, there is something "flabby" about equal opportunity *if* it involves the claim that the child of a Walmart employee has the same opportunities as a child of George Bush the Elder. In order to avoid this flabbiness I have criticized legacy and affirmative action together. To attack the latter without attacking the former is misleading, at best, and serves to continue injustice, at worst. But to admit this much is not to deny that an employer or an admissions officer is entitled to learn about, and make decisions based on, an employee's or a student's talents, skills, level of training, and level of motivation (once again, see Freeman 2007b, 129, 132, 157, 469–71).

In ideal theory, however, the goal is to get clear on what the two principles of justice would mean for a society's institutional order at the most general level. To this end Rawlsians conclude that basic liberties are never to be traded off for anything else, contra utilitarianism (see Pogge 2007, 32, 78–80, 105, 117–21, 126, 131–32). It has been the purpose of this chapter to show why it is perfectly understandable that Rawls never defended in writing either legacy or affirmative action, given the priorities examined above. It is precisely these priorities that are required to avoid the pitfalls of any system of utility, whether unrestricted or restricted.

In the less than ideal situation in which we find ourselves at present, the system of *unrestricted* utility to some extent provides the theoretical basis for the economic system. On this view, as long as gross domestic product is increasing, and as long as average utility is high when the amount of wealth is divided by the number of citizens, the intellectual heirs of Adam Smith are generally happy. One of the major problems with this approach is that no rational person would agree to it when given the choice of other alternatives behind the veil of ignorance. In short, unrestricted or average utility is too risky, and it stretches to the breaking point the strains of commitment in the original position given that one might be incarnated as someone whose formal or material rights were overridden for the sake of the aggregative reasons that are integral to utilitarianism itself. In reality there are defenders of legacy and affirmative action. But those who defend either legacy or affirmative action can do so only if they avoid the rigors of the sort of fair decision-making procedure found in the original position.

Or again, political liberals should also be opposed to the only slightly more palatable option provided by a scheme of *restricted* utility. This view, popularly known as welfare capitalism, stands in partial contrast to the laissez-faire capitalism found in a system of unrestricted utility. The problem is that the restrictions in a system of restricted utility are quite minimal. Once citizens have been rescued from the horrors of absolute poverty in welfare capitalism, the aggregative logic of utilitarianism then returns to its largely unrestricted operation. Once again, when reasonable people who desire to abide by fair terms of agreement enter the original position, and when they rationally deliberate there, they simply would not choose a scheme of utility, not even a restricted one.

As we have seen Shelby argue, the breadth and depth of Rawlsian egalitarianism, which many scholars still do not sufficiently understand, "might . . . have the effect of sharply reducing the resentment for past racial injustice" (2004, 1712), which is not to say that the past injustice should be forgotten. As the famous line from Wordsworth's immortality ode has it, regarding the need for accurate memory: what having been must ever be. The reduction of such resentment might also go hand in glove with the desire to conform to reasonable decision-making procedures. Although such resentment is not associated with defense of legacy, I have previously indicated why such a defense is even more objectionable than a defense of affirmative action. As my colleague Maria Carl once put it, it seems especially bothersome that we privilege the privileged. The hope is that Rawls's influence on the design of a just society will have its greatest influence in the century after he wrote, as was the case in the writings of Locke in the seventeenth century, Smith in the eighteenth, and Marx in the nineteenth (see Freeman 2007b, 458).

Because the system of restricted utility (i.e., welfare capitalism) fails the test of reciprocity, it is inferior to the difference principle. And we do not have to wait until a great deal of wealth is generated in a society before the priority rules and the difference principle can be implemented. This is a crucial consideration when confronted by the defenders of legacy or affirmative action, who urge us to wait until later or until the economy gets better before dismantling the preferred policies. I am arguing that we should share Rawls's optimism about our ability to instantiate the priority rules treated above, including the difference principle. Granted, on a Rawlsian basis, distribution according to moral desert is neither a feasible nor a defensible social aim (Rawls 2001, 73; 1999b, 147). But this does not mean that there is no place for desert in justice as fairness, with "desert" referring to legitimate expectations, including the expectation that one would not be disadvantaged or treated unfairly on the basis of religion, family background, race, sex, or some other arbitrary basis for admission or hiring (see Lehning 2009, 46, 50, 168, 227).

5

"ALL FOR THE GREATER GLORY OF GOD": WAS SAINT IGNATIUS IRRATIONAL?

Given the voluminous commentary on Rawls's classic *A Theory of Justice,* it is surprising that interesting arguments in that work have been left largely untouched. Section 83, "Happiness and Dominant Ends," is one that has yet to receive the attention it deserves, though it has not been entirely ignored. In conversations with various scholars, I have learned that in this section Rawls has given many readers the impression that he thinks dominant end views, like those of Saint Ignatius of Loyola, to whom he refers explicitly, are "irrational" or "mad."

Ignatius's famous version of a dominant end view is that everything we do should be for the greater glory of God (*ad majorem Dei gloriam*). This saying is not only the motto of the Jesuit order he founded but could also be seen as the motto for all theists in the Abrahamic traditions (Judaism, Christianity, and Islam), especially given that the great command in theism is to love God with one's whole heart and mind and strength (e.g., Deut. 6:5, Matt. 22:37, Mark 12:30). Much is thus at stake in the effort to understand Rawls's meaning and his apparent hyperbole. After all, in our postsecular society, it should be clear that many or most of the citizens whom Rawls would like to bring within the sweep of the overlapping consensus characterizing politically liberal societies are religious believers of some sort.

In the present chapter I will argue for three claims: (a) I will explicate Rawls's view and maintain that the charges of irrationality or madness do not apply to Ignatius's view. Here I will try to make Rawls's view clearer than Rawls himself makes it. (b) I will nonetheless defend Rawls's thesis that some other dominant end views *are* irrational or mad. And (c), I will demonstrate the political importance of the subject, which might initially seem to be quite abstruse and removed from the practical world.

INCLUSIVE ENDS VERSUS DOMINANT ENDS

The most common "inclusive end" for a human life in the history of philosophy is happiness. Rawls largely follows Aristotle in seeing happiness as consisting in the successful execution of a roughly rational plan of life that is arrived at under more or less favorable conditions. We tend to be happy when our rational plan of life is being executed to an acceptable extent. Like Aristotle, Rawls believes that happiness is not a totally rational affair, because in addition to rationality it involves luck. Rawls is also an Aristotelian in thinking that, despite the obvious subjective element in happiness, it is to be understood objectively. That is, if a person *believes* that he or she is on the way to a successful execution of a roughly rational plan of life, but is mistaken or deluded in this belief, we should consider this person unhappy regardless of his or her subjective satisfaction. A person in "fool's paradise" is not really happy. Here Rawls relies on Aristotle's *Nicomachean Ethics* (1097a–b) as well as on certain well-known secondary sources (Kenny 1966; Hardie 1965, 1968).

Happiness is an inclusive end in part because it is self-contained and is chosen for its own sake, not for the sake of something else. In this regard a person's happiness is similar to a work of art—a novel, say, or a painting. Even if a particular work of art is flawed in some ways, it has a certain completeness that allows the reader or viewer to see aesthetic value in it that contrasts with the aesthetic value found in other works of art. When a human life approaches "blessedness" (Rawls's word), it is analogous to a literary masterpiece by Faulkner or a painting by Leonardo. As Rawls puts the point, "happiness is not one aim among others that we aspire to, but the fulfillment of the whole design itself" (1999c, 482).

The question quite understandably arises: how to choose rationally among possible plans of life? Rawls is famous (or infamous) for his effort to construct a fair decision-making procedure regarding justice in an original position behind a veil of ignorance. He appeals to something similar here, in that a plan of life is one that would be chosen (albeit without the help of a community of all reasonable/rational agents) with deliberative rationality. Lucidity is required in both the original position and when choosing a plan of life. One's choice of a plan of life should stand up to critical reflection. For example, it would not be rational to decide to devote oneself to becoming a professional athlete if one were anemic and uncoordinated. Or better, because there is no single point at which one chooses one's entire plan, there are typically several key points where the most significant decisions are made, even if quotidian decisions themselves are not trivial.

After some starts and stops (it is to be hoped that the stops are not tragic), we eventually decide on a plan we most prefer without further guidance from principle. But along the way we must always consider our aims carefully if we are to achieve an acceptable degree of happiness. Rawls has us consider the deceptively simple example of planning a vacation. Should we go to Las Vegas to gamble or to New York to see museums? This is an easy choice if we are bored with gambling and enjoy paintings. The choice becomes more difficult if a museum lover is deliberating between going to see Leonardo paintings in St. Petersburg or in Krakow.

The key point here is that in exercising deliberative rationality we can narrow the scope of preferential choice (given our limitations and interests, etc.), *but we cannot limit the scope altogether.* Whitehead was fond of pointing out that the word "de-cision" literally means the "cutting off" of some possible choices so as to leave the others alive (e.g., 1978, 43). Decision involves indeterminacy. If is only *after* a decision has been made that the result is determinate. Before the decision is made there are (more or less) determinables, but nothing determinate. People have various aims, and there is no algorithmic standard that tells us exactly how to decide, as there is, for example, in the laws of long division, where we will get always the right answer so long as we keep our columns straight, subtract correctly, and so forth.

In practical deliberation there are many pauses. It is in these moments of literal *in*decision that a single, dominant end seems alluring. A dominant end is different from an inclusive end. An inclusive end like happiness still leaves us with many decisions to make, both trivial (or apparently trivial), like what to eat for lunch, and serious, like whether to change careers. By contrast, a dominant end holds out the prospect of escape from decision making because, rather than helpful heuristic devices that vaguely point the way toward a decision that is conducive to happiness, one looks for a perfectly clear and precise procedure that cannot be resisted.

To be explicit, a dominant end is like the aforementioned *algorithmic* laws of long division, which, if followed properly, always give the correct answer. In contrast, an inclusive end like happiness permits only *heuristic* devices, like the advice to mountain climbers to make sure that the next step is higher than the previous one. Usually this advice works, but not always, because sometimes (say, if one reaches a crevasse) one must go down a bit in order to find a route to the top.

A dominant end theorist understandably *wants* to avoid situations where aims conflict and where there is no infallible standard for deciding among them. But *can* we avoid such situations? Is it really that easy to reach a condition where the only difficulties in choosing a plan of life are computational, or merely involve a lack of information? Rawls is right to be skeptical here.

A dominant end theorist wants a method that the agent in question can use in order always to make a rational decision. Or, more forcefully, what is desired is a first-person procedure that is guaranteed to give the best result. But we have no procedures that meet these conditions when a plan of life, rather than basic mathematical problems, is at issue. The heuristic schemes we use in everyday life are influenced by our personal and cultural histories, and they are frequently modified. It is possible that such schemes will be rational, but there is no guarantee of this. What we can hope for is that they be minimally rational and enable us "to get by" and hold the wolf of despair at bay. There is an underappreciated pragmatic element in Rawls's thought here. His Aristotelianism is, in this regard, much like Dewey's. The schemes we use in everyday life to pursue happiness may fall short of the best we could do, but we nonetheless are justified in thinking that we are happy and that our lives are indeed worth living.

TYPES OF DOMINANT ENDS

Thus far I have said very little about the different types of dominant ends. It should be reiterated that happiness itself is not a dominant end, in that it is attained when a rational plan has been more or less executed, a plan that includes a plurality of aims, whatever these happen to be and however they happen to be ordered. If these aims are ordered in terms of certain dominant ends, however, it makes sense to say that such ends are irrational or mad, as Rawls rightly claims.

Suppose one proposes as a dominant end the acquisition and exercise of political power or the gaining of social acclaim or increasing one's material possessions (a kind of hedonism). Our considered moral judgments are at odds with these aims *when they are elevated to the status of dominant ends.* That is, each one of these proposed aims must be moderated and brought within some sort of reflective equilibrium with other ends that reasonable people accept. Indeed, it seems inhuman to propose, say, that the maximization of political power is a dominant end that could trump the political rights of others. The same is true of increasing material possessions when proposed as a dominant end that could trump the rights of others to basic goods. A dominant end by definition is lexically prior to all other aims such that seeking to advance it takes precedence over all other aims.

Rawls suggests cryptically that another problem with some dominant end views, in addition to irrationally disrupting reflective equilibrium, is that they threaten the unity of the self. By making the desire for social acclaim a dominant end, we take the rational part of the self and hide it in a corner, so to speak. Our desire to engage in reciprocal fair relations with others is relegated to a second self, as it were. Reflective equilibrium, among all of the legitimate aims that we have—the aim to be fair, the aim to have enough material possessions to exercise a rational plan of life, and so forth—requires that we resist many dominant end views.

Making the acquisition and exercise of political power a dominant end is a recipe for fanaticism. Because each of us has heterogeneous aims, the human good itself is heterogeneous. The irrationality or madness of some dominant end views consists in the subordination (or worse, eradication) of aims that, on reflection, strike us as perfectly legitimate. These dominant end views tend to disfigure the self for the sake of system.

The question arises: does Ignatius's (i.e., the theist's) version of a dominant end view necessarily lead to such a disfigurement, or worse, to irrationality or madness? Rawls is not clear on this point; the text (1999c, 485) could be read as having these charges apply only to dominant end views like the acquisition and exercise of political power, or it could be read as applying more generally to all dominant end views. It is at least possible to read Rawls as saying that dominant ends like the acquisition and exercise of political power are irrational; but, while problematic, Ignatius's dominant end is not necessarily irrational or mad. I will pursue this latter approach while admitting that Rawls's text itself is unclear regarding the extent of the charge of irrationality.

In any event, Ignatius's motto is at least problematic because we are still left with the project of figuring out how exactly to live our lives. Although Ignatius's dominant end is not irrational, as we will see below, it *is* understandably vague and ambiguous. *How* are we to glorify God if divine intentions are often left either unspecified from revelation or specified in confusing ways? In the latter respect, consider the following example: at times in scripture we are admonished to do our good deeds anonymously so that the right hand knows not what the left hand does (Matt. 6:3). In this way the good deeds are done deontologically for their own sake. But at other times we are admonished to publicly and boldly witness to the good so that we should shout from the rooftops (Luke 12:3). In this way we avoid tepidity.

There is a long tradition, especially in Catholic Christianity, of emphasizing the need to use natural *reason* to figure out exactly how we should lead our lives, choose our careers, and so on. That is, the solution to the problem of how to achieve happiness is only apparently solved by Ignatius's supposed dominant end view in that, even on his own terms, we must balance principles and pieces of evidence, and we must determine precedence. Even if we accept Ignatius's motto in the effort to achieve ultimate happiness, we must still *work* to bring about harmony among all of the complex factors involved. This need for intellectual effort indicates that his theocentric "dominant" end does not really dominate, despite the language about *all* of one's strength, and so on. It operates merely as a heuristic device to help a theist along the way.

It must be admitted that the end of furthering divine intentions *does* provide some guidance in the life of a theist, since on this basis one would, other things being equal, prefer health to sickness, honor to dishonor, and friendship to animosity. Unless, of course, sickness acts as a spur to spiritual perfection, or apparent honor spoils us, or friends lead us astray. Stranger things have happened in *theosis,* or the process of spiritual perfection. There seems to be no escape from "discernment," to use an Ignatian term (see Ignatius of Loyola, *Spiritual Exercises,* "Principle and Foundation" in the first week and "Three Occasions When a Wise and Good Choice Can Be Made" in the second week). And it is precisely this need for discernment that prevents Ignatius's dominant end view from becoming irrational or mad.

Ignatius is famous for the role of "indifference" in the effort to discern *how* to lead a life for the greater glory of God. I assume a family resemblance among Ignatian indifference, Stoic *adiaphoria,* the Buddhist "no self" doctrine, and Saint John of the Cross's *nada.* The common idea here is that we should not become attached to anything that could lead us away from ultimate happiness; in other words, we need detachment. At times, however, this effort at detachment and commendable indifference is facilitated by play, sport, or other diversions. In themselves these ludic activities do not seem to be part of the elusive dominant end: *ad majorem Dei gloriam.* But these activities, as Saint Thomas Aquinas also realized and as Rawls notes, relax the mind so that we can return to our dominant end with more vigor (Saint Thomas Aquinas, *Summa Contra Gentiles,* book 3, chapter 25; Rawls 1999c, 485; Dombrowski 2009). Various subordinate ends need to be weighed carefully in the effort to advance the nominally dominant one. A similar admonition can be found in the utilitarian tradition regarding the need to relax one's relentless efforts to ameliorate pain in the world lest one contribute to the sum of unhappiness via poor health, fatigue, and so forth.

Freeman is very helpful here in alerting us to the fact that there are two "ideal perspectives" in Rawls: the original position, which is designed to help us develop a defensible concept of justice, and deliberative rationality, which is designed to aid us in developing an appropriate concept of the good. Although the latter is nonpublic, it is not exactly private in that efforts at deliberative rationality are open to criticism, as in the person who decides that he will pursue happiness by becoming a National Basketball Association player, despite the fact that he is approaching age sixty and is five foot eleven. In *A Theory of Justice,* if not in *Political Liberalism,* stability in society is reached when there is congruence in most citizens' lives between these two ideal perspectives, when most citizens' conceptions of the good also further justice (Freeman 2007b, 265–66).

Rawls's treatment of Ignatius, however, examined above, calls into question Freeman's assertion that there is little talk of religion in *A Theory of Justice* (see Freeman 2007b, 320; also Dombrowski 2001a). Where Freeman is helpful is in emphasizing the point that reasonable people will not adopt "mad" doctrines (2007b, 367; 2007a, 53–54, 68, 73, 78) and that the main flaw of many varieties of perfectionism is that they leave little or no room for free deliberation. Or again, the relationship between teleological doctrines and deontological ones is strongly analogous to the relationship between theories that propose a single rational goal and those that deny this sort of dominance. And the problems here are not merely with religious versions of teleology but also (and perhaps primarily) with hedonism as a dominant end view.

JUSTICE

The subject of this chapter is not peripheral to the major concerns of Rawls's philosophy. The elaboration of a decision-making procedure regarding justice in an original position behind a veil of ignorance is central to *A Theory of Justice* and is assumed as background in Rawls's later books. Although a plan of life is part of what Rawls, in *Political Liberalism*, calls a comprehensive doctrine, it is nonetheless something that would be chosen with deliberative rationality. That is, although people are given considerable elbow room in a politically liberal society to choose whatever plan of life they wish, they are nonetheless constrained to do so within the bounds of justice. Likewise, in *The Law of Peoples* Rawls is clear that various peoples around the globe should be given the opportunity to have their culture flourish as long as their cultural practices would be compatible with the deliberations of the reasonable/rational contractors in the second and third original positions at the international level.

Rawls would oppose the adoption of a dominant end such as the acquisition and exercise of political power *at the expense of* the rights of others. One is not free to choose a dominant end that leads to fanaticism. Likewise, the increase of possessions as a dominant end that would have hegemony over just distribution of wealth is not acceptable owing to Rawls's second principle of justice, especially the difference principle, the idea that unequal distribution of wealth can be just only if it maximizes the long-term prospects of the least advantaged members of society. The justification of this principle centers on the idea that reasonable/rational agents would agree to it as fair.

Rawls is *not* claiming that one must engage selflessly in supererogatory actions in order to be just or happy. In fact, saints and heroes might
not even strive to be happy if they are always looking out for the interests
of others. Nonetheless, they may ironically be happy in spite of themselves by advancing the claims of justice or the well-being of others, or
by achieving the excellences for which they aim.

Obviously some religious dominant ends are as dangerous as the un-
varnished quest for power or fame or fortune. As is well known, religious
zeal is often accompanied by intolerance or injustice (see Dombrowski
2001a). But love of God does not necessarily entail misanthropy. To the
contrary. If human beings are made in the image of God, as Wolterstorff
(2008), among others, has recently argued, and as Judaism and Christianity historically claim, and as Islam implies, then literal phil-anthropy
and an Ignatian theocentrism are quite compatible.

In sum, the Ignatian belief that all that we do should be for the greater
glory of God is perfectly compatible with the Rawlsian concept of the
burdens of judgment and with justice. This is due to Ignatius's emphasis
on the need for discernment in the religious life and for rational deliberation. Neither he in particular nor theists in general are necessarily irrational or mad. But despite the compatibility between Ignatius's motto and
Rawlsian justice, one need not subscribe to Ignatius's motto, or even to
theism of a more attenuated sort, in a just society. This is especially the
case in Rawls's later writings, where there is less of a tendency to speak
of a thin notion of the good; rather, a just society is one characterized by
an overlapping consensus reached by reasonable/rational individuals (or
associations) who affirm various different thick conceptions of the good,
only some of which are theistic.

LOVE

It is not enough to argue that Saint Ignatius is not necessarily mad and
that religious believers *could* be good citizens in a just (or approximately
just) society. It is also important to point out the *positive* connections
between Rawlsian justice and the social goals of those who defend theistic metaphysics.

Because a problem of justice does not even arise unless there is a
significant difference of opinion on some serious issue, it does not make
much sense to assume that the disputing parties are perfect altruists.

Justice as fairness models the separate interests of individuals and associations that conflict in terms of the assumption of mutual disinterest in the original position. This is quite different from making the (dogmatic) claim that human beings are, by their very nature, egoistic. The parties in the original position are assumed to be mutually disinterested for the sake of method.

Here is where Rawls's method differs quite markedly from the utilitarian one. The latter appeals to an impartial sympathetic spectator in order to achieve objectivity. But there is another way to achieve this goal, in that objectivity is more likely to be reached in decisions made in the original position. "Instead of defining impartiality from the standpoint of a sympathetic observer, we define impartiality from the standpoint of the litigants themselves" (Rawls 1999c, 165). That is, utilitarians tend to confuse impersonality with impartiality.

The issue here should be of intense interest to religious believers who privilege agapic love when dealing with social issues. If agapic love involves the desire to advance the other person's good, a difficulty arises when the claims of various persons to be loved conflict. One can legitimately wonder what "love of mankind" could possibly mean. As Rawls puts it, "benevolence is at sea as long as its many loves are in opposition" (1999c, 166).

Love or benevolence is here seen as a second-order notion in that it seeks to advance the good(s) of beloved individuals with the good(s) in question already given. If the distinctness of persons is respected, even loving agents need conceptual help. This help is ably provided by Rawls's two principles of justice. Love is guided by what reasonable/rational individuals themselves would agree to in a fair initial situation. "We now see why nothing would have been gained by attributing benevolence to the parties in the original position" (1999c, 167). To be sure, the sense of justice and love are compatible. Indeed, they can easily work in tandem even if love is wider than the sense of justice in that the former prompts supererogation that is not necessarily encouraged by the latter.

The development of love can be traced through the morality of authority (where, ideally, parents love their children and children learn to love the parents in return), the morality of association (where fellow feeling for persons outside of the family is enhanced), and the morality of principles, including the two principles of justice agreed to in the original position. These principles secure for all citizens those goods that would be desired for others in a society held together by mutual benevolence

(Rawls 1999c, 405–19). Here the sense of justice and agapic love mutually reinforce each other. Just as love for another makes one vulnerable, in that the lover feels the other's sufferings vicariously, so also the fraternal bonds that characterize reasonable people in a just society entail that we agree to bear one another's burdens, especially if they are due to arbitrary losses in the natural and social lotteries (502–3).

In sum, agapic love is a natural attitude that both undergirds the effort to approximate a just society, on the one hand, and extends the effort beyond what is required in its exhortation to supererogation, on the other. In other words, it *frames* justice. One who utterly lacked a sense of justice would probably be a person who felt that he or she was never loved and hence felt the need selfishly to resist all appeals to reasonableness (Rawls 1999a, 100–110). For all our sakes it is to be hoped that such people remain few in number.

FREEMAN AND RELIGION

The complexity of these issues is made apparent by appeal to Freeman's treatment of the relationship between political liberalism and religion, a treatment at times more harsh than Rawls's. For example, Freeman argues that very often the poor learn to accept their subservience to the rich through a misguided religion and that oppressive religious education very often spoils children *as future citizens* (2007b, 179, 257). Freeman may be correct on these points. But I think he is premature in claiming that the thesis that God created the realm of value leads to false belief. As I see things, the Rawlsian view ought to include a bracketing of this thesis in politics so as to leave open the possibility that religious believers might be right on this point, or at least that abstract objects like values or concepts in logic and mathematics are "intradeically" contained in the mind of God if not outright created by God (see Freeman 2007b, 322, 328; see also Dombrowski 2005, chapter 3). Further, Freeman seems to identify religious belief with a commitment to miracles, an afterlife, and the existence of spiritual beings (2007b, 351). In the following chapter I argue that these commitments characterize some types of religious belief, but not others. That is, one must be careful not to offer a caricature or straw-man version of religious belief based on its least defensible exemplifications.

To be fair to Freeman and to avoid a caricature of *his* position, it should be noted that he sees the sense of justice as an extension of the natural sentiment of love, as detailed above. It is precisely this sentiment that is the cornerstone of religious ethics at its best. And it is this extension that makes it possible (or, in a society characterized by stability for the right reasons, likely) that religious believers be politically reasonable (2007b, 254, 350).

The key is that citizens "bracket" meta-issues in politics. One of the reasons why Rawls uses the phrase "comprehensive doctrine" in *Political Liberalism* is to underscore the fact that this bracketing needs to occur not only with religious believers but with those who defend nonreligious comprehensive doctrines as well. That is, "comprehensive doctrine" is meant to be much more general than "religion." Because of the political parity between religious and nonreligious comprehensive doctrines, however, it is hard to understand Freeman's claim that freedom of conscience is worth more to atheists than to religious believers. Conscientious objectors who oppose war on religious grounds, for example, might think otherwise. The hope is that *all* reasonable people, whatever their comprehensive doctrine, could converse *together* on the subject of political justice so that there would not be entirely separate conversations among Catholics, Jews, atheists, and so on (see Freeman 2007b, 62, 354; 2007a, 39; see also Weithman 1991).

Freeman is at his best on the subject of religion when he distinguishes between moral autonomy in general and political autonomy in particular. If liberal freedoms are not merely individual freedoms (as many of liberalism's detractors claim) but also associational freedoms, then there are good reasons for thinking that the government should be reluctant to intrude too much into family matters. The issue is notoriously difficult, not least because the family is arguably different from most other associations in that one does not choose to join it. But one legitimate requirement on the part of the government is that the education of children include familiarity with democratic values, especially *political* autonomy. This is not to say that families committed to traditionalist religious beliefs have to inculcate in their children a *comprehensive moral* autonomy. After all, they might sincerely believe that ultimately all that we do is for the greater glory of God. And they are not necessarily irrational or mad in having such a belief. Indeed, many religious believers might view comprehensive moral autonomy as a conceit. But in a just society children need to learn that neither apostasy nor conversion is a crime (Freeman 2007b, 238–39, 320, 362; 2007a, 95–96, 184–85, 304–5; see also Maritain 1940, 1951).

It will no doubt be objected that Rawlsians are utopian (in the pejorative sense) in thinking that, despite vast differences in opinion among citizens at the level of comprehensive doctrine, we can nonetheless reach agreement regarding justice at the political level. An initial response to this objection is that we already, not in some utopian world but in the actual one that we inhabit, have evidence of overlapping consensus regarding justice at the political level. In Freeman's helpful terms, justice may be *secondary* to the vision of God or the utilitarian greatest good, and so forth (depending on the comprehensive doctrine in question), but it is nonetheless *final* when civil disputes arise among reasonable citizens. It is final because overlapping consensus is not a compromise or a (Hobbesian) bargain but rather arises out of, or can be embedded in, citizens' various comprehensive doctrines. In Freeman's instructive terms, "Kantians can accept the political conception for reasons of ethical autonomy . . . ; utilitarians, because they might well believe (truly or falsely) that justice as fairness is the best workable approximation to the requirements of social utility in a democracy; a liberal Catholic, because she sees justice as fairness as compatible with natural law; and pluralists, because they accept the public justification of justice as fairness as sufficient moral argument, not in further need of justification in more comprehensive terms. In each case, the political conception is affirmed for reasons distinctive to each doctrine" (2007a, 191; see also 2007b, 327–28, 367, 369). This initial response to the objection that disagreement at the level of justice is likely to follow disagreement at the level of comprehensive doctrine will be supplemented momentarily. The point here is that the thesis that overlapping consensus is utopian is contradicted by the facts in existing liberal democracies (see Weithman 1994a, 1994b).

One of the greatest advances Rawls made in the transition from *A Theory of Justice* to *Political Liberalism* is that in the later work he offers a more convincing explanation of "stability for the right reasons." The earlier work sometimes gives the impression that each citizen shares the same liberal comprehensive doctrine with other citizens such that stability is a function of "congruence" between one's liberal conception of *the* good and one's conception of justice or the right. In short, congruence means that it is quite simply rational to be reasonable. In the later book, however, Rawls entertains no such unrealistic hopes; overlapping consensus starts from the assumption that reasonable citizens affirm incompatible comprehensive doctrines and that a stable society can be obtained when there is sufficient overlap on political questions among the plurality of comprehensive doctrines. That is, one need not have one argument for Catholics, another for Jews, and still another for agnostics, in that reasonable people in all three of these groups can speak the same language of justice (Freeman 2007a, 170, 182).

It is odd that communitarian critics of Rawls are unhappy with his concept of overlapping consensus. The oddness stems from the eclectic character of communitarianism itself, which includes defenders of Aristotelianism, Thomism, Hegelianism, feminism, cultural relativism, and so on, including both right-wing and left-wing views (Alasdair MacIntyre and Benjamin Barber, respectively). Granted, all communitarians share a commitment to perfectionism in general, but which perfectionism should we privilege? Given the plurality of comprehensive doctrines defended by communitarians, it seems best to side with Freeman and to distinguish rather sharply between the sort of cooperation found at the communal, associational level and the sort of metacommunal cooperation that is required for a just society (2007b, 506; 2007a, 6, 269).

Freeman is astute in noticing that Rawls's method of avoidance does not necessarily mean that the content of a religious comprehensive doctrine can *never* be brought to bear on public discourse. That is, Rawls was not a pure exclusivist like Richard Rorty. Rather, one can bring a religious (or nonreligious) comprehensive doctrine to bear on public discourse as long as the duty of civility is met. This duty requires, however, that we translate the way we might speak at the associational level into its rough equivalent at the level of public discourse. If there is no rough equivalent, then it is best to remain silent. An example of this translation proviso is conveniently provided by Martin Luther King, who sometimes spoke of a time when all of *God's* children would walk together in a society free of racial discrimination and at other times spoke in terms that would be acceptable to all reasonable citizens. But even when he used religious language, reasonable agnostics knew what he had in mind and agreed with him; hence he supported public reason even when he invoked his (Christian) comprehensive doctrine. Attentive listeners to King very often were willing to do the translation themselves and found the task relatively easy (Freeman 2007b, 380–81; 2007a, 200, 215; see also Weithman 1997).

In addition to being bound by the duty of civility, which is a moral rather than a legal duty in that King could have exercised his legal right to speak religiously without making any effort to fulfill the translation proviso, one is also obviously bound to a moral *and* legal duty to respect human rights. For example, a Muslim society that punishes women for talking with men violates human rights and is hence unjust (Freeman 2007a, 267). This point should be emphasized if only because many scholars have mistakenly concluded that because Rawls is not willing to force-feed the *liberal* rights appropriate for a democratic society to the rest of the world (see, for example, his treatment of mythical Kazanistan in *The Law of Peoples*), he has withdrawn support from *human* rights. Nothing could be further from the truth, in that it is appropriate to insist that basic human rights be respected in every part of the globe, including those societies governed by consultation hierarchies that privilege one religious comprehensive doctrine over other comprehensive doctrines (Freeman 2007b, 430).

Although Rawls is not willing to force liberal rights on nonliberal peoples (i.e., he wisely avoids the violence necessarily connected to messianic liberalism), this does not mean that he thinks of consultation hierarchies as exhibiting public reason. As Freeman rightly emphasizes, basing laws on the Koran would not be an exercise in public reason even in Saudi Arabia, where the vast majority of people are Muslim. This is because public reason is a characteristic only of a democratic people. In a democracy the state enforcement of a religion is unjust, as is persecution of those who defend heterodox versions of that religion (see An-Na'Im 1990; Freeman 2007b, 383).

But public reason would not necessarily be at odds with government vouchers that make it possible to attend religiously affiliated schools, so long as public goods were served. For example, hundreds of thousands of students have attended Catholic schools in New York City, including a great number of African Americans who were not Catholic, such that without this alternative the already overburdened public school system in that city would have been pushed to the breaking point. Even if public funds should not be spent on the explicitly religious part of the education provided in religiously affiliated schools, there is no reason to prevent public funds from being used for science education or for nursing programs in religiously affiliated universities, especially at a time when there is a shortage of nurses (Freeman 2007b, 381, 391; 2007a, 220).

The claims made in the previous paragraph are not meant to compromise the freestanding character of justice as fairness. Justice is a module that can be fit into various comprehensive doctrines: Kantian, utilitarian, natural law, several forms of perfectionism, and so forth (Freeman 2007a, 188–89). So if public funding for religiously affiliated schools in New York City were to be seen as just, such funding would have to fit as a module into more than religious comprehensive doctrines. That is, if such funding were just, then reasonable agnostics would have to agree to do their part to bring it about. Once again, by the time he wrote *Political Liberalism* Rawls had come to see more clearly that a stable society was the result less of congruence between a single liberal conception of the good and justice than of overlap among several conceptions of the good and justice. The latter sort of stability requires public reasons in ways that the former sort of stability would find superfluous. The key concerns are that one's nonpublic conception of the good not outmuscle one's public commitment to justice, and that stability not rest on citizens' second-best choices, as Freeman rightly emphasizes (2007b, 368; 2007a, 192, 198–203).

As before, Freeman's language is a bit harsher than Rawls's own regarding the place of religion in a politically liberal society, even if he is helpful in supporting the argument that there is nothing inherently irrational or mad about religious belief. His negative attitude toward religion is shown in a small way in his denigration of monasticism. He says that a mendicant monk has more wealth than a poor person if he has access to a library, cloistered gardens, and so on (2007b, 153). Actually Freeman seems to be describing some version of Benedictine monasticism found in the Cistercians, Carthusians, or Trappists, rather than a mendicant order like the Franciscans or Dominicans. Further, the mendicants were not monks (literally, to be one alone) but friars. Admittedly the point is a small one.

More worrisome is that sometimes Freeman speaks as if he wishes to equate religious belief with a literal belief in the biblical account of creation. When this tendency surfaces in his writing, he opposes religious belief to "Darwinian evolution." The term is problematic because it could refer either to some form of the hypothesis of evolution or to a necessarily reductionist materialist version of that hypothesis. The latter is certainly at odds with almost all varieties of religious belief. But there is a long tradition, from Teilhard de Chardin to John Haught and John Cobb, that seeks to reconcile religious belief with evolution, indeed to show that the latter is required by the former (see Teilhard 2003; Haught 2000, 2003; Cobb 2008). By ignoring this tradition Freeman creates a vacuum that could unfortunately be filled with the claim that religious belief is irrational or mad, or at least is at odds with our best available scientific theories (2007b, 309, 327–28, 387, 507; 2007a, 236). We can do better, I think.

But Freeman is especially helpful in his treatment of the political problem of abortion. Whatever one's view of the morality of abortion, in a politically liberal society such a view must be compatible with public reason, in that the state's use of coercive power in a pluralistic society must, in order to be fair, be justified in terms that all reasonable citizens can understand and plausibly accept. That is, such a justification ought not to be in terms of a particular comprehensive doctrine that simply could not be accepted by the person coerced. As is now well known, Rawls isolates three major values at work in the abortion debate: respect for human persons, equality of women, and the reproduction over time of liberal society (see Freeman 2007b, 386; also, e.g., Rawls 2001, 117; 1996, 243–44; 1997, 798–99). I will focus on the first two of these values in the assumption that the abortion debate does not figure significantly in the issues of how to produce new citizens (this is relatively easy) and how to educate them into liberal citizenship (which is a bit harder, but the effort is not hindered by legalized abortion).

Freeman's achievement consists in his emphasizing that on a Rawlsian basis there is a transfer of the burden of proof in the political debate about abortion. To outlaw abortion *simpliciter* would severely restrict the freedom of women who wish to have abortions; hence there is a presumption against restrictive abortion laws because these laws militate against the equality of women. The question is, can abortion opponents meet the burden of proof by justifying restrictive abortion laws in terms of public reason?

Granted, respect for human persons is a value on a par with the equality of women with men. (Indeed, the latter can be seen as a species of the former, which can be seen as the more generic value.) And all reasonable parties agree that pregnant women are human persons. But there is reasonable disagreement as to whether fetuses in the early stages of pregnancy are human persons. For example, Saints Augustine and Thomas Aquinas were delayed (rather than immediate) hominization theorists (see Dombrowski 2000), and many contemporary individuals follow these thinkers in being skeptical about the personhood of the early fetus. Although the *metaphysical* status of the early fetus is not a political question, the fact that there is significant disagreement regarding the metaphysical status of the early fetus among otherwise reasonable citizens *does* have political consequences. One of these is the aforementioned injustice of having one's own comprehensive doctrine trump others in a condition of reasonable pluralism when one's comprehensive doctrine has implications for (or is seen, perhaps mistakenly, to have implications for) the abortion debate.

Because the denial of abortion rights puts a severe restriction on certain women's freedom, and because many citizens cannot see the early fetus as a *political* patient with sentiency, or even with the proximate potential to develop sentiency (even a sperm cell all by itself has some remote potential to develop sentiency), abortion should be permitted in the early stages of pregnancy. There must be some compelling case for the political status of the early fetus in order to severely restrict a woman's freedom to have an abortion. And this case has not been forthcoming (Freeman 2007b, 405–11), even if Rawls himself seemed to commend Joseph Bernardin, who was the Catholic archbishop of Chicago, for trying to provide such a case (however inadequately) in terms that were within the bounds of public reason (1996, lvi). Many reasonable people are just not convinced that the (amazing) genetic makeup of a fertilized egg, for example, makes it a moral or political patient.

But Freeman is also correct to insist that owing to the functioning of a central nervous *system* in the third trimester (in contrast to unconnected nerve cells that develop earlier in pregnancy), restrictions on late abortions are politically defensible. That is, reasonable citizens are in universal agreement that sentiency makes one a political patient of *some* sort, although there may be disagreement about the extent of political protection that ought to be afforded sentient beings. But if a being is not sentient (i.e., if it has no experiences of its own), it is hard to see how it could be the subject of political concern (see Freeman 2007b, 414; 2007a, 42). The important question is whether there are sufficient public reasons for overriding the political value of women's equality. And the prochoice argument is that there is no acceptable case within public reason for the personhood of the early fetus (Freeman 2007a, 247; see also Pogge 2007, 89); hence the burden of proof on the prolife side is not met (cf. George 1997; Haldane 1996).

POGGE'S CONTRIBUTION

Thomas Pogge enables us to understand the relationship between political liberalism and religion at a deeper level still. It might be an embarrassment for a *comprehensive* liberal to discover that many or most Catholics support political liberalism, but *political* liberals greet this fact with elation. We should not overemphasize the restrictions that religious believers have to follow in order to be democratic citizens. Rather, we should encourage religious believers to find within their own traditions the grounds for respecting citizens in general, even if they do not share one's own comprehensive doctrine. For example, liberal Catholicism ought not be seen as Catholicism-lite but rather as Catholicism understood at a deeper level. Given the pacific character of the life of Jesus, there was always something fishy about versions of Christianity that encouraged or required intolerance and violence (Pogge 2007, 41, 57, 82, 140; Dombrowski 1991; Yoder 1972; see also Weithman 2002).

Pogge addresses the issue in what I see as a remarkable passage. He imagines what a liberal religious believer might say to herself just before engaging in political discourse:

> I know which political outcome would be pleasing to God. But I cannot demonstrate this knowledge to my fellow citizens in a way that is accessible to them. Forcing the correct decision on them without being able to show them why it is correct—this would not be a service to God but would, on the contrary, negate their God-given freedom. Urging them to accept this truth without being able to show them its grounds would deny them the respect they are due as equally endowed with reason by our Creator. In public political discourse, I should therefore appeal to the values and facts all citizens can acknowledge together and should support whatever political decisions seem most reasonable on this basis. Some such political decision will go against religious truths. But, from the divine standpoint, this is a lesser evil than denying other citizens the respect due them as creatures endowed with reason and conscience. (2007, 141)

This fictional piece of reasoning captures well the claim that religious believers respect the duty of civility not *in spite of* their religious beliefs but *because of* them.

Pogge, more than Freeman, emphasizes the point that on the Rawlsian view one is not only *permitted* to provide deeper foundations for the
freestanding character of justice as fairness as a political doctrine; one is
encouraged to do so. That is, the broadening of overlapping consensus is
not at all at odds with deepening one's justification of respect for persons. Perhaps it will be objected that if someone thinks that he or she is
in possession of religious truth, this person will have less reason than
others to observe the duty of civility. The proper response to this objection, as Pogge again rightly notes, is that reasonable religious believers
affirm that the duty of civility simply *is* part of religious truth (2007, 144,
159, 176–77, 186–87, 195). In effect, most religious believers in democratic societies have come to see religious intolerance as an attenuated
(at best) or distorted (at worst) form of religious belief itself.

It changes things quite a bit when "public reason" is distinguished
from "secular reason," when the latter means the reasoning found in
nonreligious comprehensive doctrines. With this distinction in place we
can see that religious believers are not required to "assimilate," in the
pejorative sense of this term, although they are required to exhibit allegiance to liberal political values. To put the point sharply, the omnicom-
petent laicist state is unjust, but we should resist not only this kind of
state but also those religious comprehensive doctrines that completely
reject the modern world, including its liberal political values, among
them the political autonomy of citizens, including women (see Lehning
112, 120, 130, 161, 163, 171, 203; see also Rawls 1999c, 186–87).

6

RAWLSIAN RELIGION

Between 1890 and the mid-twentieth century, liberal theology was the dominant force in the field. It is therefore quite ironic that when Rawls, the greatest liberal thinker since Mill, wrote his senior undergraduate thesis in Princeton's philosophy department in 1942, but on a topic in theology, he defended a view that was heavily influenced by the neo-orthodox reaction against liberal theology.

The purpose of this chapter is to examine this senior thesis from the perspectives of both liberal theology and Rawls's own later political liberalism. In the former effort I will indicate the sort of liberal theology that Rawls *could* have defended (but did not), given some of his own commitments. I will also claim that some of the neo-orthodox arguments that he actually did offer in this early work make his posthumously published essay from the 1990s, "On My Religion," more intelligible than it might otherwise be. I am indebted to Thomas Nagel, Joshua Cohen, Robert Adams, and Eric Gregory for their work in making available to scholars these two works—one very early and one very late—that relate in a crucial way to Rawlsian religion.

In his instructive three-volume study of the history of liberal theology in America, Gary Dorrien characterizes liberal theology as a collection of views based on reason and experience rather than on external authority like the Bible or the papacy. This basis places liberal theology between orthodox authority religion, on the one hand, and secular disbelief, on the other. Any authority the Bible has within liberal theology is located *within* Christian (or some other religious) experience, rather than as an external force that compels belief (see Dorrien 2009). Further, because the basis for this type of theology comes from reason and experience, it is also usually associated with a sort of political progressivism.

Several of these features of liberal theology—the emphasis on reason and the desire to find compatibility between religion and science, suspicion regarding external authority, political progressivism, and so on—therefore seemingly commend themselves to the very early Rawls. But given these features of liberal theology, and given liberal theology's dominance, it is not surprising that by the end of the 1920s fundamentalists had largely broken away from mainline Protestant denominations and opted for sectarianism by forming a vast array of new denominations with their own Bible colleges.

Liberal theology flourished in at least three major academic centers. First, evangelical liberalism was taught at Union Theological Seminary in New York; second, personalism was dominant at Boston University; and third, religious naturalism was centered at the University of Chicago. The latter two deserve special notice, given Rawls's own personalism in his senior thesis and his critical account of naturalism, respectively.

It is ironic that the Kantianism of the personalist school at Boston University did not influence the very early Rawls, given the personalism in his senior thesis and his later Kantian view of the human person. One can easily imagine, counterfactually, the very early Rawls warming up to the personalism of Borden Parker Bowne and Edgar Brightman, as did Martin Luther King, who received his doctorate in theology from Boston University. In this environment it was axiomatic that Christianity was concerned primarily with the care of persons seen as ends in themselves and not with propping up an outgrown mythology. As is well known, Rawls's treatments of civil disobedience and pacifism in *A Theory of Justice* and his insistence that one be ignorant of one's race behind the veil of ignorance were all very much influenced by his admiration for Martin Luther King.

Or again, the religious naturalism of the Chicago School, which turned toward process theology around the time that Rawls was writing his senior thesis, emphasized several themes that one might assume, again counterfactually, would have been agreeable to the very early Rawls: dialogue between religion and science, intrareligious conversation (which shows a family resemblance to the tolerance among competing comprehensive doctrines found in the later Rawls), and rich debate on subjects in rational theology. In chapter 1, I tried to show the fruitfulness of interpreting Rawls's own method of reflective equilibrium in process terms that are compatible with the best in Alfred North Whitehead and Charles Hartshorne.

By way of contrast with what was going on at these three centers of liberal theology, Princeton Theological Seminary, which operated in close proximity to the very young Rawls, was not friendly to liberal theology. Indeed, it welcomed Emil Brunner to campus as a celebrity just before Rawls was a student there (Adams 2009, 29). It is against this historical background and with these ironies in mind that I now turn to Rawls's text.

NEO-ORTHODOXY AND LIBERAL THEOLOGY

Several themes in the very young Rawls suggest the heavy debt he owed to neo-orthodox thinkers like Brunner, Philip Leon, and Anders Nygren. The most important of these is a hostility toward the influence of Greek philosophy on Christianity. As Rawls put it sharply, "An ounce of the Bible is worth a pound (possibly a ton) of Aristotle" (2009, 107, 254). We should keep this in mind when we consider his later remarks on fideism. Apparently Rawls believed throughout his life that it was doubtful whether natural or rational theology could tell us very much; and the very early Rawls thought that all we needed to know about God could be found in the Bible (111, 263). His main objection to the influence of the Greeks on religion in particular, and to natural or rational theology in general, was that these approaches did not tell us anything about God as a *person*, which for the very early Rawls was a significant defect (224).

This surprising opposition, for lack of a better word, to human *autonomy* in religion goes hand in glove with his opposition to Pelagianism, the early Christian view that human beings could earn salvation by their own merit (see Cohen and Nagel 2009, 18; Rawls 2009, 170–71, 229, 231). (And it also prefigures his famous suspicions regarding the role of merit in a just society found in *A Theory of Justice,* as we will see.) Robert

Adams and Eric Gregory have done masterly work in detailing the neo-orthodox influences on Rawls as well as the sense of disillusionment of neo-orthodox thinkers like Karl Barth with the liberal or modernizing trend in Christianity from the time of Friedrich Schleiermacher in the nineteenth century. This disillusionment led neo-orthodox thinkers, including Rawls, to rethink Saint Augustine's appropriation of Plato for the purposes of religion (Adams 2009, 93–94, 97; Gregory 2007).

Rawls is nonetheless clear that there are reasons to believe that God exists and that such a belief is not mere fancy. And he also implies that Plato's late dialogues need not have had the negative influence on religion that the early (and middle) dialogues had, but he gives no explicit indication of what in the late dialogues earns them this exemption. One possible contribution of the late Plato dialogues is that they encourage us to think of God in terms that avoid dangerous anthropomorphism, as when God is described as angry (Rawls 2009, 85, 113, 137, 226).

Although the very early Rawls wants to avoid the anthropomorphism associated with divine anger, the cornerstone of his view is nonetheless that God is personal and that personal existence is at odds with the thesis that God is strictly permanent and not changing, pure being and not becoming, and immutable in every respect (2009, 246). Something changeless in every respect would more closely resemble a rock than a person. This consideration would seem to push Rawls toward liberal theology, specifically toward the process theistic version of liberal theology in vogue at the University of Chicago and elsewhere. But Rawls stops short of this position by once again associating something negative (in this case, the notion of God as a completely static being) with Greek philosophy. As I see things, this view of the Greek philosophers is more popular among scholars than it should be, given all of the evidence to the contrary (see Dombrowski 2005).

In any event, Rawls is certainly correct that if God is a personal being who loves creatures, then this God could not be a completely static being or an unmoved mover if the love in question is even remotely analogous to any love with which we are familiar. If someone we love previously did not suffer but now starts to suffer, we are moved by the suffering. Preeminent love would not so much eliminate this movement as exhibit it in the best way possible. Indeed, if an omnibenevolent God loves *all* creatures in ideal fashion, then this being would be the *most* moved mover (see Rawls 2009, 88). Contrary to the God of neo-orthodoxy, the God of liberal process theology is the Eros of the universe in the sense that the process God acts as a lure toward a better social world and a more beautiful natural world than we have at present (cf. Adams 2009, 46, 62). Admittedly, although Rawls's personalism would seem to be at home with this liberal process view of God (and with his eventual political liberalism), it is not the liberal process God that he defends in neo-orthodox fashion.

Or better, there are moments when Rawls gestures in the direction of liberal theology, despite his dominant neo-orthodox tendencies. We see this in his rejection of divine immutability (see again 2009, 246; see also Adams 2009, 90–91). We see it also in his statement that community and personality are "the inner core of the universe" and that "the personal quality of the universe" is "intimate" (2009, 107–8, 112, 216). Although Rawls apparently did not read Martin Buber, he may have indirectly learned about Buber's I and Thou through Brunner (Adams 2009, 97), as is evidenced in the following classification of relations: (a) personal and communal relations are between an "I" and an "I"; (b) natural relations are between an "I" and an "it"; and (c) causal relations are between an "it" and an "it" (2009, 114–15). The biggest problem with the views of Saints Augustine and Thomas Aquinas, as the very early Rawls sees things, is that they reduce the relationship between human beings and God to natural relations. That is, they compromise the personal nature of God by making God into an immutable "it" that cannot be moved. Here Rawls's criticism of traditional (or classical) theism is remarkably close to that found in Hartshorne. For the very early Rawls, the universe is made up of personal relations. But by seeing the universe as a whole as personally, divinely ordered, Rawls has unwittingly played into the hands of those liberal process theologians who see God as the soul for the whole body of the world.

Hartshorne famously defended this Platonic view for decades, which would have been available to Rawls had he been exposed to cutting-edge liberal theology, as he would have been had he attended the University of Chicago, say. My point here is not to trash Princeton but to indicate how really odd it is that Rawls, the eventual political liberal par excellence, never seemed to have seriously considered liberal theology. He did read Origen, whom he regarded as the greatest of the Alexandrian theologians, but he does not seem to have noticed Origen's belief in God as the Platonic World Soul, as the soul for the whole body of the universe. Rawls does seem to have been a hylomorphist rather than a dualist regarding human nature at the time of his senior thesis, but it seems that he was not aware of the sort of cosmic hylomorphism entailed in the (Hartshornian) liberal belief in God as the World Soul (see Rawls 2009, 126, 133; also Dombrowski 1996, chapter 3). Nonetheless he comes close to this view, not only in his stance regarding the universe as personal and communal but also in his linking of this stance with several well-known texts from Saint Paul on the universe as the mystical *body* of Christ (e.g., 1 Cor. 6:13–15; see Rawls 2009, 138). That is, Rawls comes close to cosmic hylomorphism even if he ultimately retreats to cosmic dualism, to a belief in God as a disembodied spirit who hovers above the natural world.

ANTICIPATIONS OF LATER POLITICAL VIEWS

It is easy to isolate those points where the very early Rawls says things that are at odds with his later political philosophy. Prominent among these points is the claim that religion and ethics (presumably including that part of ethics that is concerned with political philosophy) cannot be separated (2009, 116, 205). Hence the very early Rawls assumed that the best way to get to a just society was through one comprehensive doctrine (Christianity), which violates political liberalism in a major way. That is, the very early Rawls is too muscular in his communitarianism. Another difference between the very early Rawls and what came later is the absence in the very early Rawls of any discussion of communal institutions, despite the frequent references to community (see Adams 2009, 67–68).

And the very early Rawls defends the doctrine of original sin, whereas later he rejects this doctrine because he sees it as contradicting the belief that we can construct a society that approximates justice (2009, 171–73, 191, 263). This is odd. Granted, the literal (overly pessimistic) version of this doctrine, whereby each new human being inherits the sin of Adam and is thereby flawed, is indefensible for various reasons. But an analogical interpretation of it would seem to be compatible with some important parts of Rawls's own theory of justice. For example, the very need for the original position is due in part to the pervasiveness of bias in most people's initial conceptions of justice (see Rawls 1999c, 452–55). That is, Rawls could have benefited from the qualified defense of original sin offered by Langdon Gilkey (1966) of the Chicago School.

Despite these wide divergences from Rawls's later political philosophy, there are more lines of continuity than one might expect between the very early Rawls and the famous parts of Rawls that developed later. In this regard I would like to make nine points.

(1) Rawls alerts us from the start that his view *does* have implications for political theory (2009, 110). (2) And he exhibits from the start what Nussbaum finds objectionable in Rawls: a (Kantian) bifurcation between natural relations and personal relations (119). (3) Opposition to egoism (or "egotism," as the very early Rawls uses the term, which he borrows from Leon) also characterizes Rawls's work throughout his career, whether the egoism in question is descriptive or prescriptive. (4) This also leads the very early Rawls to oppose social contract theory, which is not as strange as it sounds given that at this stage in his career he identified this theory with the Hobbesian version based on threat advantage (122–23, 126, 189, 217, 227, 229; see also Cohen and Nagel 2009, 13; Adams 2009, 85).

(5) In addition to preparing the way for his later opposition to egoism, the very early Rawls does the same for his later opposition to (even supposedly noble) lying (2009, 155, 195; 1999c, 398; Dombrowski 1997b, 2004c) and to (6) fascism or other political philosophies that basically take one comprehensive doctrine and ram it down the throats of unwilling others (see Rawls 2009, 198, 207, 212). On this point neo-orthodox thinkers like Leon would have supported Rawls (see Adams 2009, 39). (7) Further, the very early Rawls treats in detail the conversion experience of Saint Paul (2009, 232–39), an experience that he later uses to defend the thesis that neither apostasy nor conversion is a political crime (e.g., 1996, 32).

(8) Rawls's opposition to meritocracy is well known (although the precise nature of this opposition is still debated, as we saw in chapter 4 regarding legacy and affirmative action). The very early Rawls prepares the way for this opposition by arguing that merit is beside the point in establishing community; indeed, it could be seen as sinful if by "sin" we mean that which is ultimately corrosive of community, as the very early Rawls thinks (2009, 230). It should be noted that the very early Rawls's Christian opposition to merit is continuous with his later Kantianism in that Kant himself noticed that birth is not a deed of the one who is born, such that the undue influence of natural and social contingencies should be resisted.

This critique of merit shows the influence of the Protestant side of the old debate between Protestant and Catholic thinkers regarding the inefficacy of "works" in partial contrast to "faith," the latter term referring to that which ultimately contributes to community, on Rawls's usage. But it also shows affinity with the theological concept of grace that is central to almost all Abrahamic theists (perhaps not the Pelagians). Rawls asks rhetorically, "who paid for your education . . . who . . . provided you with good fortune that you did not need to steal . . . ?" Much of what we accomplish in life is a result of (divine or other) gifts; thus to concentrate on merit is "to turn Christianity upside down" (2009, 240–41; also Adams 2009, 67, 86, 88). Likewise, we might say that a politically liberal society is turned upside down by a concentration (or at least by an overconcentration) on merit. This is true in part because reasonable contractors behind a veil of ignorance agree to share one another's fate.

(9) Finally, the very early Rawls's remarks on love help to illuminate what he says in A Theory of Justice about the relationship between love (or benevolence) and justice. Many religious believers are turned off by Rawls's theory of justice because, even though Rawls's social contract is not based on Hobbesian cunning, they see it nonetheless as cold and overly "rational," in the pejorative sense of the term (such that it prohibits love and other partial affections). One can imagine mutual anathemas being thrown back and forth: in Rawls there is much talk about justice but nothing about love, whereas in the Christian scriptures, say, there is a great deal of talk about love but little about justice.

Actually, both accusations are false. The accusation against religious ethicists that they are overly agapistic is due to the fact that, largely under the influence of neo-orthodox (and other) scholars such as Nygren, the multitudinous instances of dike and its cognates in the Christian scriptures have typically been translated as "righteousness" or "uprightness," whereas this same term and its cognates when they appear in Plato's dialogues are always translated as "just" or "justice," as Wolterstorff correctly notes. That is, the impression that religious ethics is not focused on justice is to a considerable extent the result of the vagaries of translation rather than of anything integral to Christianity in particular or to Abrahamic theism in general. Admittedly, this impression is accurate to the extent that neo-orthodox thinkers like Nygren (and the very early Rawls) try to distance themselves as much as possible from Greek thought, including Greek thought regarding justice. There has to be some reason, after all, why scriptural translators often render dike and its cognates as "righteousness" rather than as "justice."

The accusation against Rawls is also inaccurate, as we saw in the previous chapter. In the design of an appropriately defined decision-making procedure, Rawls cannot stipulate that the participants in the original position are perfectly loving agents, for he would then be criticized for stacking the deck in his favor. Nor can he stipulate that these participants are selfish to the core, for such beings would be incapable of justice. Rather, he adopts the moderate position that they are capable of reciprocity by way of judicious deliberation. The important point here is that the mutually disinterested agents of construction found in the original position *when constrained by* the veil of ignorance produce a conception of justice that is very close to what would result if a just society were planned by purely loving agents! (For example, the difference principle is strongly analogous to the preferential option for the poor urged by the contemporary Catholic Church and by the World Council of Churches.) This is one of the best-kept secrets in Rawlsian philosophy, despite Rawls's explicit statement of this point (1999c, 128–29).

In the very early Rawls it is clear that the ability to respond to love is what enables one to enter into any sort of community with others (2009, 148, 251), including, we are to assume, what will later become the meta-community of liberal citizens in an approximately just society. Thus it is not strictly accidental that love and justice coincide in their results in Rawls's magnum opus. He makes a related point in that work about the typical development of a child from the morality of authority (where the child learns to respond to being loved by parents), to the morality of association, to the morality of principles. The impulse toward love and justice runs deep in Rawls, from his very early period to his latest works, even if the religious manifestation of love starts to look more and more supererogatory from the time of *Political Liberalism* on. But the fact that he never repudiated the difference principle, say, indicates that, in a peculiar way, his very early religious ethics was sedimented into his thought until the end. Although Rawls defended the difference principle until the end (see 1999c, xiv), it must be admitted that by the time he wrote the preface of the revised edition of *A Theory of Justice* in 1990, he was willing to reach rapprochement with a limited number of other ways of defending the distribution of wealth.

Or again, it is a well-known fact about political life in the United States that candidates in primary elections tend to emphasize what Rawls calls their comprehensive doctrines, whereas in general elections they tend to try to appeal to as many people, and hence to as many comprehensive doctrines, as possible. (I have Evan Hershmann to thank for this point.) Although the motivation here is primarily strategic rather than philosophical, it is nonetheless unwitting confirmation of a Rawlsian belief in public reasonableness, in contrast, say, to a more Hobbesian or Straussian version of political life dominated by calculative rationality or cunning, respectively. We ought not to be surprised that people generally *want* to get along with others, quite apart from strategic considerations.

THE *IMAGO DEI* HYPOTHESIS

In chapter 1 I alluded to the oddity that someone who is influenced by some version of reductionism, and who views a human being as nothing other than protoplasmic stuff that is the accidental by-product of blind evolutionary history, might nonetheless belong to Amnesty International. It is precisely this oddity that leads Wolterstorff to ask *why* we should view human beings as politically free and equal and worthy of moral respect. As far as I can tell, there are three stages in Rawls's career relative to this question.

First, the very early Rawls gives abundant evidence of support for the thesis that human beings are made in the image of God; hence there is something heroic or semidivine about a human life that makes it special. On this basis, it makes perfect sense to pay one's dues to Amnesty International. As an image of God, a human being is thereby capable of entering into community with the same in that a personal God is in the divine nature itself communal; hence to be made in the image of such a being is to share in some fashion this communal nature. Further, it is because human beings are made in the image of God that Rawls thinks that they are not merely natural beings and hence can be held accountable for their actions (2009, 113, 121, 193, 203, 205–6, 208, 219; see also Cohen and Nagel 2009, 11).

This defense of the *imago Dei* hypothesis in the very early Rawls enables us to better understand his anthropocentrism as discussed in chapter 3. Although I wonder if the implications of this hypothesis lie more in the direction of theocentrism and away from anthropocentrism, it is clear that Rawls himself goes in an anthropocentric direction, in that not to see ourselves as superior to nonhuman animals would be to show ingratitude toward God for making us, in contrast to nonhuman animals, in the divine image. For the very early Rawls, if this image were destroyed, a human being would be merely an animal, a purely natural being incapable of community. Hence it would be a mistake, he thinks, to hold that human progress should be judged in terms of society's ability to advance a human being's animal pleasures and to ameliorate a human being's animal pains. As he forthrightly puts the point, "man is not biological, but communal; he is not an animal but a person" (2009, 139, 207, 209, 215, 217–18).

Second, there is the Kantian view of the human person in *A Theory of Justice*. Given what the very early Rawls says in defense of the *imago Dei* hypothesis, we can now see further evidence of why it makes sense for Wolterstorff, Zuckert, and Dworkin (see chapter 1) to suspect that behind the Rawlsian view of free and equal persons lies something like Locke's view, or a natural rights view, or something else that has a family resemblance to the Judeo-Christian view of the human person that derives from Genesis. And it also makes sense, as we have seen, for Goldmann to suspect that behind the Kantian view of the human person as an end in itself (adopted by Rawls in *A Theory of Justice*) lies theistic metaphysics. As Franklin Gamwell and Habermas and Griffin and others have correctly noted, the human rights movement has been heavily insured; it has been living off the capital of the religious ages for quite some time now, but not necessarily by paying the premium required in terms of an explicit defense of theism (see Dombrowski 2006c; see also Berkowitz 1999; Griffin 2007, chapter 7; Gamwell 1995, 2002, 2005).

Hence, third, it is understandable why Rawls in *Political Liberalism* moves away from the Kantian view of the human person in *political* philosophy, although one gets the impression that Rawls's own comprehensive *moral* doctrine remained Kantian (and hence implicitly theistic) until the end, including a Kantian conception of the human person.

I have tried to argue that this third stage need not be as problematic as Wolterstorff and other scholars think it is. From a *political* point of view, theists like myself are free *both* to indicate why we think it makes sense to defend the thesis that rational human beings, and sentient beings of whatever species, deserve moral respect, *and* to ask religious skeptics who are reductionists to provide the justificatory warrant for their Amnesty International membership. But this latter freedom should be exercised at the associational level rather than at the political one, in that the deep metaphysical reasons for one's political beliefs are themselves not political. Further, I tried to show in chapter 1 how the Rawlsian method of reflective equilibrium itself eliminates the requirement that there be absolutely secure starting points in political philosophy, say, those that would be provided by the certainty that human beings are made in the image of God. That is, even with insecure starting points, the back-and-forth movement of reflective equilibrium leads to a conception of justice as fairness that is as secure as a reasonable being would, in good conscience, want it to be, given the fact of reasonable pluralism.

RAWLS'S RELIGION AND RAWLSIAN RELIGION

Joshua Cohen and Thomas Nagel are correct to notice in Rawls "a deeply religious temperament that informed his life and writings" (2009, 5). We have seen his deep religiosity in his Princeton thesis. And his posthumously published essay "On My Religion" (apparently written in the early 1990s) is also compatible with this view of Rawls as deeply religious, although some explication of the text is required to see why this is so (see the helpful article by Reidy 2010).

Rawls tells us in this essay that his mother was an Episcopalian and his father a Methodist, and that during his childhood his family attended an Episcopalian church. He was conventionally religious until his last two years at Princeton, when it seems fair to say that he was converted to a more intense level of Christian belief and even thought about entering the seminary. This is evidenced in his treatment of conversion in the undergraduate thesis, which is the best part of that work, according to Adams (2009, 83). But in "On My Religion" Rawls also tells us that, as a result of his experiences in World War II, he abandoned orthodoxy.

Here there is a certain ambiguity, and it seems that Rawls wants to keep it that way: "And since then I have thought of myself as no longer orthodox, as I put it, which expresses it vaguely enough, as my views have not always remained the same" (2009, 261). What remains unclear is whether Rawls ever abandoned theism altogether. To cite an example close at hand, I think of myself as a theist, but not as an orthodox one.

Rawls cites three incidents that led him to abandon orthodox Christianity while he was in the army in the war. First, he speaks of a sermon he heard by a Lutheran pastor in which the pastor said that God aimed Allied bullets at the Japanese and in turn protected the Allies from Japanese bullets. In the second incident, a sergeant needed Rawls and his friend to perform two tasks: to give blood that was needed for a badly wounded soldier and to engage in reconnaissance of certain Japanese positions. Because only Rawls had the right blood type, he was chosen for the first task and his friend was given the second. Rawls's friend, Deacon, was killed on the mission. And third, Rawls was understandably shaken when he saw an army film that first made him aware of the horrors of the Holocaust.

As a result of these three incidents, Rawls quite understandably began to see grave defects in the traditional (or classical) theism with which he was familiar as a result of reading neo-orthodox thinkers. And as a result of these defects he understandably abandoned orthodox Christianity. But he does not tell us that he abandoned theism. Indeed, he goes out of his way to say that even after these incidents took place his "fideism remained firm" (2009, 263).

It should be noted that this Rawlsian pattern of (a) orthodox belief in youth that is (b) shattered in the face of both chance events (as in the Deacon incident) and horrendous evil (as in the Holocaust) but (c) yields to religious faith of a heterodox sort is similar to the pattern also followed by the great figures of liberal process theism. The death of Whitehead's son in World War I and Hartshorne's experience as a medic in that war come to mind as in extremis events that radically altered the religious beliefs of the figures in question (see, e.g., Hartshorne 1990, chapter 6). Rawls's ambiguity on these matters consists largely in his difficulty in distinguishing between heterodox theism and nontheism (see, e.g., 2009, 269).

This is not the place to defend the neoclassical theism of the liberal process thinkers. Suffice it to note that it is a hallmark of this sort of theism that the divine attribute of omnipotence comes in for heavy criticism (e.g., Whitehead 1961, chapter 5, 20; Hartshorne 1984b). It is precisely this attribute that precludes an understanding of chance events like Deacon's death. If God is omnipotent, as neo-orthodox thinkers assert and as the very young Rawls believed (see 2009, 252), it is unclear whether anything *could* occur by chance in that everything that happens would be either sent by God or at least permitted by God for some purpose. And it is when God is seen as omnipotent that the nastiest version of the theodicy problem arises (see Griffin 1976).

My point here is that it makes sense for Rawls to remain ambiguous in "On My Religion." Having abandoned traditional (or classical) theism, and yet finding himself believing, but without the intellectual resources provided by some version of liberal neoclassical theism, he had no alternative but to be ambiguous or vague. Once again, he does not eliminate the vagueness by declaring himself an agnostic or atheist.

Quite apart from Rawls's own religious beliefs or nonbeliefs is the Rawls*ian* approach to religion that has been my main concern in this book. This approach is primarily moral (or more precisely, political) rather than metaphysical in character. But a clean cut between metaphysical and practical issues in religion cannot be made. For example, if one holds the traditional (or classical) theistic view that God is omniscient *in the sense that* God knows already in minute detail and with absolute assurance what will happen in the future, then the doctrine of predestination (found in different forms in Saints Augustine and Thomas Aquinas, Luther, and Calvin) follows. But the practical consequence of predestination is "terrifying," according to the very late Rawls, and it leads to a view of God as a "monster" (2009, 264).

Once again, it is unfortunate that Rawls seems to be unaware of the similar critique of this version of omniscience, and of the practical difficulties therein, in liberal process thinkers (e.g., Hartshorne 1970; Shields and Viney 2003). Here omniscience is interpreted in somewhat different terms. It consists in ideal knowledge of everything that can be known: past actualities as already actualized, present realities in their presentness (subject to the limitations detailed by physicists), and future possibilities or probabilities *as possibilities or probabilities*. That is, to claim to know a future possibility or probability as already actualized is to misunderstand the future. This view of time as asymmetrical, wherein one's relation in the present to the past is radically different from one's relation in the present to the future, preserves the freedom that Rawls thinks is essential for political agency. Indeed, the loss of such agency implied in a belief in predestination he understandably sees as terrifying.

Although there can be no perfectly clean cut between metaphysical and practical issues in religion (in that the former bleed into the latter), it can nonetheless be stated with confidence that it is the practical consequence of religious belief in politics that is of prime importance from a Rawlsian point of view. From this vantage point, intolerance is the great curse of much religious belief, both historically and to some extent today as well. But the denial of religious freedom is also a great evil, as is well known in politically liberal circles. One of the defects in much religious belief that is not often noticed is its tendency to overemphasize individual salvation or purity. Rawls cites the overly scrupulous views of those

Germans who resisted Hitler but who hesitated to assassinate him. Although assassination of political leaders is a crime in just war theory, Rawls thinks that the larger picture of civilized life renders such scruples trivial by comparison (2009, 265). Here his view of religion is unfortunately trumped by his view of supreme emergency, as detailed in chapter 2. On my view, however, deontologists ought not to be faulted for having scruples.

It seems to me that the overall contours of the Rawlsian approach to the place of religious belief in a condition of reasonable pluralism are nonetheless on the mark. Along with Rawls we should do our best to continue to embody the best in, and to eliminate the defects in, Locke's *A Letter Concerning Toleration* and Jean Bodin's *Colloquium of the Seven About Secrets of the Sublime*. The latter work is sadly not as well known as the former, although both works greatly influenced Rawls. Bodin was a sixteenth-century Catholic thinker who argued for the political importance of toleration. Further, he did not argue for this position as a member of a persecuted religious minority but defended religious toleration as "an aspect and consequence of the *harmony of nature* as expressed in God's creation" (Rawls 2009, 266, emphasis added).

In effect, Rawlsian religion consists in a surprising attempt to revitalize the natural law tradition in contrast to the tradition of divine command theory, as we also saw in chapter 1 regarding Rawlsian natural rights. Atheists and agnostics would be in a precarious position if they lived in a society ruled by divine command theorists, but they need not fear living under those whose touchstone is the natural ability to reason, possessed by religious believers and nonbelievers alike (see Rawls 2009, 267–69). Or again, in theory the natural law position can be rendered compatible with the best in Rawlsian religion, even if in practice natural law theory has often been appropriated by those whose political views are hardly liberal.

One common view is that "liberalism" and "modernity" go together such that as a society modernizes, religious belief declines to the vanishing point (see Zafirovski 2007). It counts in favor of Rawlsian religion that it sees religious belief as something other than a vanishing act. In a related way, for quite some time I have noticed that when most scholars think of the relationship between science and religion, as well as the relationship between politics and religion, they immediately think of *conflict* (see Dombrowski 2001a, 157). But these scholars tend to exaggerate these conflicts. In order to work our way to a more sober view, it might

be profitable to expand our historical vision in the way that a wise diplo-
mat uses a large-scale map as a precaution against panic and against a
misunderstanding of the general peace among nations.

Granted, it was first science in the early modern period that faced
change with an open-mindedness that has incrementally worked its way
into politics (starting with Bodin and Locke and others) and religion as
well. It should also be granted that religious ideas tend to develop more
slowly than those in politics and especially science. But this should not
dampen the hope that eventually religious belief will become widely associated with both the best scientific explanations of the natural world and
the best available features of a just society (see Whitehead 1925, 1926,
1978). The large-scale map metaphor leads me to think that such a hope
is part of a Rawlsian "realistic utopia," with both words in this oxymo-
ronic expression requiring equal emphasis.

REFERENCES

Adams, Robert. 2009. "The Theological Ethics of the Young Rawls and Its Background." In Rawls, *A Brief Inquiry into the Meaning of Sin and Faith with "On My Religion,"* ed. Thomas Nagel, 24–101. Cambridge: Harvard University Press.

Alexander, Larry. 1985. "Fair Equality of Opportunity: John Rawls' (Best) Forgotten Principle." *Philosophy Research Archives* 11:197–207.

Allen, Anita. 2004. "Race, Face, and Rawls." *Fordham Law Review* 72:1677–96.

Allen, Robert. 2004. "Rawlsian Affirmative Action: Compensatory Justice as Seen from the Original Position." http://www.bu.edu/wcp/Papers/Soci/SociAlle.htm.

Anderson, Elizabeth. 2004. "Animal Rights and the Values of Nonhuman Life." In *Animal Rights: Current Debates and New Directions,* ed. Cass Sunstein and Martha Nussbaum, 277–98. Oxford: Oxford University Press.

An-Na'Im, Abdullahi Ahmed. 1990. *Toward an Islamic Reformation.* Syracuse: Syracuse University Press.

Appiah, Kwame Anthony. 2002. "Racisms." In *The Right Thing to Do,* 3d ed., ed. James Rachels, 264–81. New York: McGraw-Hill.

Arneson, Richard. 1999. "Against Rawlsian Equality of Opportunity." *Philosophical Studies* 93:77–112.

Aron, Raymond. 1966. *Peace and War.* Trans. Richard Howard and Annette Baker Fox. Garden City, N.Y.: Doubleday.

Ball, Howard. 2000. *The Bakke Case: Race, Education, and Affirmative Action.* Lawrence: University Press of Kansas.

Baltzell, E. Digby. 1964. *The Protestant Establishment: Aristocracy and Caste in America.* New York: Random House.

Barber, Benjamin. 1998. *A Passion for Democracy.* Princeton: Princeton University Press.

Becker, Lawrence. 2005. "Reciprocity, Justice, and Disability." *Ethics* 116:9–39.

Berkowitz, Peter. 1999. *Virtue and the Making of Modern Liberalism.* Princeton: Princeton University Press.

Bodin, Jean. 1975. *Colloquium of the Seven About Secrets of the Sublime.* Trans. Marion Leathers Daniels Kuntz. Princeton: Princeton University Press. (Orig. pub. 1588.)

Bowne, Borden Parker. 1908. *Personalism.* Boston: Houghton Mifflin.

Brightman, Edgar. 1940. *A Philosophy of Religion.* New York: Prentice Hall.

Brink, David. 1987. "Rawlsian Constructivism in Moral Theory." *Canadian Journal of Philosophy* 17:71–90.

Brown, Peter. 1988. *The Body and Society: Men, Women, and Sexual Renunciation in Early Christianity.* New York: Columbia University Press.

Brunner, Emil. 1929. *The Theology of Crisis.* New York: Scribner's.

Callicott, J. Baird. 1989. *In Defense of the Land Ethic.* Albany: State University of New York Press.

Carcieri, Martin. 2010. "Rawls and Reparations." *Michigan Journal of Race and Law* 15:267–316.

Cobb, John, ed. 2008. *Back to Darwin: A Richer Account of Evolution.* Grand Rapids, Mich.: Eerdmans.

Cohen, Andrew. 2007. "Contractarianism, Other-Regarding Attitudes, and the Moral Standing of Nonhuman Animals." *Journal of Applied Philosophy* 24:188–201.

Cohen, Joshua, and Thomas Nagel. 2009. "Introduction." In Rawls, *A Brief Inquiry into the Meaning of Sin and Faith with "On My Religion,"* ed. Thomas Nagel, 1–23. Cambridge: Harvard University Press.

Cureton, Adam. 2008. "A Rawlsian Perspective on Justice for the Disabled." *Essays in Philosophy* 9. http://commons.pacificu.edu.eip.vol9/iss1/.

Daniels, Norman. 1979. "Wide Reflective Equilibrium and Theory Acceptance in Ethics." *Journal of Philosophy* 76:256–82.

———. 1996. *Justice and Justification: Reflective Equilibrium in Theory and Practice.* New York: Cambridge University Press.

———. 2003. "Democratic Equality: Rawls's Complex Egalitarianism." In *The Cambridge Companion to Rawls,* ed. Samuel Freeman, 241–76. New York: Cambridge University Press.

DePaul, Michael. 1988. "The Problem of the Criterion and Coherence Methods in Ethics." *Canadian Journal of Philosophy* 18:67–86.

Dombrowski, Daniel. 1984a. *The Philosophy of Vegetarianism.* Amherst: University of Massachusetts Press.

———. 1984b. "Vegetarianism and the Argument from Marginal Cases in Porphyry." *Journal of the History of Ideas* 45:141–43.

———. 1984c. "Was Plato a Vegetarian?" *Apeiron* 18:1–9.

———. 1990. "Two Vegetarian Puns at *Republic* 372." *Ancient Philosophy* 9:167–71.

———. 1991. *Christian Pacifism.* Philadelphia: Temple University Press.

———. 1996. *Analytic Theism, Hartshorne, and the Concept of God.* Albany: State University of New York Press.

———. 1997a. *Babies and Beasts: The Argument from Marginal Cases.* Chicago: University of Illinois Press.

———. 1997b. "Plato's 'Noble' Lie." *History of Political Thought* 18:565–78.

———. 1997c. "Process Thought and the Liberalism-Communitarianism Debate." *Process Studies* 26:15–32.

———. 1998. "Rawls and Animals." *International Journal of Applied Philosophy* 12:63–77.

———. 2000. *A Brief, Literal, Catholic Defense of Abortion.* Chicago: University of Illinois Press.

———. 2001a. *Rawls and Religion: The Case for Political Liberalism.* Albany: State University of New York Press.

———. 2001b. "The Replaceability Argument." *Process Studies* 30:22–35.

———. 2002. "Rawls and War." *International Journal of Applied Philosophy* 16:185–200.

———. 2004a. *Divine Beauty: The Aesthetics of Charles Hartshorne.* Nashville: Vanderbilt University Press.

———. 2004b. "Nussbaum, the Ancients, and Animal Entitlements." *Modern Schoolman* 81:193–214.

———. 2004c. "On the Alleged Truth About Lies in Plato's *Republic.*" *Polis* 21:93–106.

———. 2005. *A Platonic Philosophy of Religion: A Process Perspective.* Albany: State University of New York Press.

———. 2006a. "'All for the Greater Glory of God': Was St. Ignatius Irrational?" *Logos* 9:109–17.

———. 2006b. "Is the Argument from Marginal Cases Obtuse?" *Journal of Applied Philosophy* 23:223–32.

————. 2006c. *Rethinking the Ontological Argument: A Neoclassical Theistic Response.* New York: Cambridge University Press.

————. 2009. *Contemporary Athletics and Ancient Greek Ideals.* Chicago: University of Chicago Press.

Dorrien, Gary. 2001. *The Making of American Liberal Theology.* Vol. 1, *Imagining Progressive Religion, 1805–1900.* Louisville: Westminster John Knox Press.

————. 2003. *The Making of American Liberal Theology.* Vol. 2, *Idealism, Realism, and Modernity, 1900–1950.* Louisville: Westminster John Knox Press.

————. 2006. *The Making of American Liberal Theology.* Vol. 3, *Crisis, Irony, and Postmodernity, 1950–2005.* Louisville: Westminster John Knox Press.

————. 2009. "The Crisis and Necessity of Liberal Theology." *American Journal of Theology and Philosophy* 30:3–23.

Doyle, Michael. 1983. "Kant, Liberal Legacies, and Foreign Affairs." *Philosophy and Public Affairs* 12:205–35, 323–53.

Dreben, Burton. 2003. "On Rawls and Political Liberalism." In *The Cambridge Companion to Rawls,* ed. Samuel Freeman, 316–46. New York: Cambridge University Press.

Dworkin, Ronald. 1977. *Taking Rights Seriously.* Cambridge: Harvard University Press.

Ebertz, Roger. 1993. "Is Reflective Equilibrium a Coherentist Model?" *Canadian Journal of Philosophy* 23:193–214.

Elliot, Robert. 1984. "Rawlsian Justice and Non-Human Animals." *Journal of Applied Philosophy* 1:95–106.

Freeman, Samuel. 2007a. *Justice and the Social Contract: Essays on Rawlsian Political Philosophy.* New York: Oxford University Press.

————. 2007b. *Rawls.* New York: Routledge.

Frey, R. G. 1983. *Rights, Killing, and Suffering.* Oxford: Blackwell.

Friedman, Marilyn. 2000. "John Rawls and the Political Coercion of Unreasonable People." In *The Idea of Political Liberalism,* ed. Victoria Davion, 16–33. Lanham, Md.: Rowman and Littlefield.

Fuchs, Alan. 1981. "Duties to Animals: Rawls' Alleged Dilemma." *Ethics and Animals* 2:83–87.

Gamwell, Franklin. 1995. *The Meaning of Religious Freedom.* Albany: State University of New York Press.

————. 2002. *Democracy on Purpose: Justice and the Reality of God.* Washington, D.C.: Georgetown University Press.

———. 2005. *Politics as a Christian Vocation*. New York: Cambridge University Press.

George, Robert. 1997. "Public Reason and Political Conflict: Abortion and Homosexuality." *Yale Law Journal* 106:2475–2504.

Gilkey, Langdon. 1966. *Shantung Compound*. New York: Harper and Row.

Gjelsvik, Tore. 1979. *Norwegian Resistance, 1940–1945*. Montreal: McGill-Queen's University Press.

Goff, Edwin. 1976. "Affirmative Action, John Rawls, and a Partial Compliance Theory of Justice." *Cultural Hermeneutics* 4:43–59.

Goldmann, Lucien. 1971. *Immanuel Kant*. Trans. Robert Black. London: NLB Press.

Graham, Kevin. 2010. *Beyond Redistribution: White Supremacy and Racial Injustice*. Lanham, Md.: Lexington Books.

Gregory, Eric. 2007. "Before the Original Position: The Neo-Orthodox Theology of the Young John Rawls." *Journal of Religious Ethics* 35:179–206.

Griffin, David Ray. 1976. *God, Power, and Evil: A Process Theodicy*. Philadelphia: Westminster.

———. 2001. *Reenchantment Without Supernaturalism: A Process Philosophy of Religion*. Ithaca: Cornell University Press.

———. 2007. *Whitehead's Radically Different Postmodern Philosophy*. Albany: State University of New York Press.

Habermas, Jurgen. 2002. *Religion and Rationality: Essays on Reason, God, and Modernity*. Cambridge: MIT Press.

Haldane, John. 1996. "The Individual, the State, and the Common Good." *Social Philosophy and Policy* 13:59–79.

Hardie, W. F. R. 1965. "The Final Good in Aristotle's Ethics." *Philosophy* 40:277–95.

———. 1968. *Aristotle's Ethical Theory*. Oxford: Clarendon Press.

Hare, R. M. 1999. "Why I Am Only a Demi-Vegetarian." In *Singer and His Critics*, ed. Dale Jamieson, 233–46. Oxford: Blackwell.

Hartshorne, Charles. 1948. *The Divine Relativity*. New Haven: Yale University Press.

———. 1953. *Philosophers Speak of God*. Chicago: University of Chicago Press.

———. 1970. *Creative Synthesis and Philosophic Method*. LaSalle, Ill.: Open Court.

———. 1984a. *Creativity in American Philosophy*. Albany: State University of New York Press.

———. 1984b. *Omnipotence and Other Theological Mistakes*. Albany: State University of New York Press.

———. 1990. *The Darkness and the Light*. Albany: State University of New York Press.

Haught, John. 2000. *God After Darwin: A Theology of Evolution*. Boulder: Westview Press.

———. 2003. *Deeper Than Darwin: The Prospect for Religion in the Age of Evolution*. Boulder: Westview Press.

Henning, Brian. 2005. *The Ethics of Creativity: Beauty, Morality, and Nature in a Processive Cosmos*. Pittsburgh: University of Pittsburgh Press.

Huffman, Tom. 1993. "Animals, Mental Defectives, and the Social Contract." *Between the Species* 9:20–26.

Kenny, Anthony. 1966. "Happiness." *Proceedings of the Aristotelian Society* 66:93–102.

Kershaw, Ian. 1987. *The "Hitler Myth": Image and Reality in the Third Reich*. New York: Oxford University Press.

———. 1999. *Hitler: 1889–1936*. New York: W. W. Norton.

Keynes, John Maynard. 1920. *The Economic Consequences of the Peace*. New York: Harcourt, Brace, and Howe.

Kittay, Eva. 1997. *Love's Labor: Essays on Women, Equality, and Dependency*. New York: Routledge.

Korsgaard, Christine. 1996. *Creating the Kingdom of Ends*. New York: Cambridge University Press.

Lamb, David. 1987. *The Arabs*. New York: Random House.

Lehning, Percy. 2009. *John Rawls: An Introduction*. New York: Cambridge University Press.

Leon, Philip. 1935. *The Ethics of Power*. London: George Allen and Unwin.

Locke, John. 1983. *A Letter Concerning Toleration*. Indianapolis: Hackett. (Orig. pub. 1689.)

Macedo, Stephen. 1995. "Liberal Civic Education and Religious Fundamentalism: The Case of God v. John Rawls." *Ethics* 105:468–96.

MacIntyre, Alasdair. 1984. *After Virtue*. Notre Dame: University of Notre Dame Press.

Mandle, Jon. 2009. *Rawls's "A Theory of Justice": An Introduction*. New York: Cambridge University Press.

March, Andrew. 2009. *Islam and Liberal Citizenship: The Search for Overlapping Consensus.* New York: Oxford University Press.

Maritain, Jacques. 1940. *Scholasticism and Politics.* Trans. Mortimer Adler. New York: Macmillan.

———. 1951. *Man and the State.* Chicago: University of Chicago Press.

Mayer, Jane, and Alexandra Robbins. 1999. "How George W. Made the Grade." *New Yorker,* November 8, 29–32.

Mendus, Susan. 1999. "The Importance of Love in Rawls's Theory of Justice." *British Journal of Political Science* 29:57–75.

Morgenthau, Hans. 1978. *Politics Among Nations: The Struggle for Power and Peace.* 5th ed. New York: Knopf. (Orig. pub. 1951.)

Morris, Randall. 1991. *Process Philosophy and Political Ideology.* Albany: State University of New York Press.

Nagel, Thomas. 1979. *Mortal Questions.* New York: Cambridge University Press.

———. 2003a. "John Rawls and Affirmative Action." *Journal of Blacks in Higher Education* 39:82–84.

———. 2003b. "Rawls and Liberalism." In *The Cambridge Companion to Rawls,* ed. Samuel Freeman, 62–85. New York: Cambridge University Press.

Nozick, Robert. 1974. *Anarchy, State, and Utopia.* New York: Basic Books.

Nussbaum, Martha. 1986. *The Fragility of Goodness.* Cambridge: Cambridge University Press.

———. 1995. *Women, Culture, and Development.* Oxford: Clarendon Press.

———. 1999. *Sex and Social Justice.* New York: Oxford University Press.

———. 2000a. "The Costs of Tragedy: Some Moral Limits of Cost-Benefit Analysis." *Journal of Legal Studies* 29:1005–36.

———. 2000b. *Women and Human Development.* Cambridge: Cambridge University Press.

———. 2001a. "Animal Rights: The Need for a Theoretical Basis." *Harvard Law Review* 114:1506–49.

———. 2001b. "Disabled Lives: Who Cares?" *New York Review of Books,* January 11, 34–38.

———. 2001c. *Upheavals of Thought: The Intelligence of Emotions.* Cambridge: Cambridge University Press.

———. 2003. "Rawls and Feminism." In *The Cambridge Companion to Rawls,* ed. Samuel Freeman, 488–520. New York: Cambridge University Press.

———. 2004a. "Beyond 'Compassion and Humanity': Justice for Non-human Animals." In *Animal Rights: Current Debates and New Directions*, ed. Cass Sunstein and Martha Nussbaum, 299–320. Oxford: Oxford University Press.

———. 2004b. *Hiding from Humanity: Disgust, Shame, and the Law*. Princeton: Princeton University Press.

———. 2006. *Frontiers of Justice: Disability, Nationality, Species Membership*. Cambridge: Harvard University Press.

Nygren, Anders. 1982. *Agape and Eros*. Trans. A. G. Herbert and Philip Watson. Chicago: University of Chicago Press. (Orig. pub. 1930–36.)

Obama, Barack. 2004. *Dreams from My Father: A Story of Race and Inheritance*. New York: Crown. (Orig. pub. 1995.)

Palmer, Claire. 2010. *Animal Ethics in Context*. New York: Columbia University Press.

Petrow, Richard. 1974. *The Bitter Years: The Invasion and Occupation of Denmark and Norway, April 1940–May 1945*. New York: Morrow.

Pincus, Steve. 2009. *1688: The First Modern Revolution*. New Haven: Yale University Press.

Pitcher, George. 1965. "Emotion." *Mind* 74:326–46.

———. 1995. *The Dogs Who Came to Stay*. New York: Dutton.

Pogge, Thomas. 1989. *Realizing Rawls*. Ithaca: Cornell University Press.

———. 1999. "A Brief Sketch of Rawls's Life." In *Development and Main Outlines of Rawls's Theory of Justice*, ed. Henry Richardson, 1–15. New York: Garland.

———. 2007. *John Rawls: His Life and Theory of Justice*. Oxford: Oxford University Press.

Pojman, Louis. 1992. "The Moral Status of Affirmative Action." *Public Affairs Quarterly* 6:181–206.

Rachels, James. 1990. *Created from Animals: The Moral Implications of Darwinism*. Oxford: Oxford University Press.

Rawls, John. 1996. *Political Liberalism*. Paperback ed. New York: Columbia University Press. (Orig. pub. 1993.)

———. 1997. "The Idea of Public Reason Revisited." *University of Chicago Law Review* 64:765–807.

———. 1999a. *Collected Papers*. Ed. Samuel Freeman. Cambridge: Harvard University Press.

———. 1999b. *The Law of Peoples*. Cambridge: Harvard University Press.

———. 1999c. *A Theory of Justice*. Revised ed. Cambridge: Harvard University Press. (Orig. pub. 1971.)

———. 2000. *Lectures on the History of Moral Philosophy.* Ed. Barbara Herman. Cambridge: Harvard University Press.

———. 2001. *Justice as Fairness: A Restatement.* Ed. Erin Kelly. Cambridge: Harvard University Press.

———. 2007. *Lectures on the History of Political Philosophy.* Ed. Samuel Freeman. Cambridge: Harvard University Press.

———. 2009. *A Brief Inquiry into the Meaning of Sin and Faith with "On My Religion."* Ed. Thomas Nagel. Cambridge: Harvard University Press.

Regan, Tom. 1981. "Duties to Animals: Rawls' Dilemma." *Ethics and Animals* 2:76–82.

———. 1983. *The Case for Animal Rights.* Berkeley and Los Angeles: University of California Press.

Reidy, David. 2010. "Rawls's Religion and Justice as Fairness." *History of Political Thought* 31:309–44.

Robertson, Esmonde, ed. 1971. *The Origins of the Second World War.* London: Macmillan.

Rorty, Richard. 1999. *Philosophy and Social Hope.* New York: Penguin.

Rowlands, Mark. 1997. "Contractarianism and Animal Rights." *Journal of Applied Philosophy* 14:235–47.

Russow, Lilly-Marlene. 1992. "Animals in the Original Position." *Between the Species* 8:224–29, 232–33.

Scanlon, Thomas. 1998. *What We Owe to Each Other.* Cambridge: Harvard University Press.

———. 2003. "Rawls on Justification." In *The Cambridge Companion to Rawls,* ed. Samuel Freeman, 139–67. New York: Cambridge University Press.

Schapiro, Tamar. 2006. "Kantian Rigorism and Mitigating Circumstances." *Ethics* 117:32–57.

Seagrave, Stephen. 2009. "Rawls's Humean Moment." Paper delivered at the American Political Science Association Convention, Toronto, September 5.

Shelby, Tommy. 2004. "Race and Social Justice: Rawlsian Considerations." *Fordham Law Review* 72:1697–1714.

Sher, George. 1979. "Reverse Discrimination, the Future, and the Past." *Ethics* 90:81–87.

Shields, George, and Donald Viney. 2003. "The Logic of Future Contingents." In *Process and Analysis,* ed. George Shields, 209–46. Albany: State University of New York Press.

Shiffrin, Seana Valentine. 2004. "Race, Labor, and the Fair Equality of Opportunity." *Fordham Law Review* 72:1643–75.

Singer, Peter. 1979. *Practical Ethics.* Cambridge: Cambridge University Press.

Stern, J. P. 1975. *Hitler: The Fuhrer and the People.* Berkeley and Los Angeles: University of California Press.

Stokes, Gale. 1993. *The Walls Came Tumbling Down: The Collapse of Communism in Eastern Europe.* New York: Oxford University Press.

Stoltzfus, Nathan. 1992. "Dissent in Nazi Germany." *Atlantic Monthly,* September, 87–94.

Taylor, A. J. P. 1962. *The Origins of the Second World War.* New York: Atheneum.

Taylor, Robert. 2009. "Rawlsian Affirmative Action." *Ethics* 119:476–506.

Teilhard de Chardin, Pierre. 2003. *The Human Phenomenon.* Trans. Sarah Appleton-Weber. Sussex, UK: Sussex Academic Press.

Thomas, Keith. 1983. *Man and the Natural World.* New York: Pantheon.

Timberg, Robert. 2007. *John McCain: An American Odyssey.* New York: Free Press.

Tomhave, Alan. 2008. "Comments on Dombrowski's 'Rawls and War.'" Paper delivered at the Northwest Philosophy Conference, University of Oregon, December 8.

Vandeveer, Donald. 1979. "Of Beasts, Persons, and the Original Position." *Monist* 62:368–77.

Van Parijs, Philippe. 2003. "Difference Principles." In *The Cambridge Companion to Rawls,* ed. Samuel Freeman, 200–240. New York: Cambridge University Press.

Walzer, Michael. 1983. *Spheres of Justice.* New York: Basic Books.

———. 2004. *Arguing About War.* New Haven: Yale University Press.

———. 2006. *Just and Unjust Wars.* 4th ed. New York: Basic Books. (Orig. pub. 1977.)

Weithman, Paul. 1991. "The Separation of Church and State." *Philosophy and Public Affairs* 20:52–65.

———. 1994a. "Rawlsian Liberalism and the Privatization of Religion." *Journal of Religious Ethics* 22:3–28.

———. 1994b. "Taking Rites Seriously." *Pacific Philosophical Quarterly* 75:272–94.

———, ed. 1997. *Religion and Contemporary Liberalism.* Notre Dame: University of Notre Dame Press.

———. 2002. *Religion and the Obligations of Citizenship.* New York: Cambridge University Press.

White, Zachary. 2009. "Transformative Toleration." Paper delivered at the American Political Science Association Convention, Toronto, September 2.

Whitehead, Alfred North. 1925. *Science and the Modern World.* New York: Macmillan.

———. 1926. *Religion in the Making.* New York: Macmillan.

———. 1961. *Adventures of Ideas.* New York: Free Press. (Orig. pub. 1933.)

———. 1978. *Process and Reality.* Corrected ed. New York: Free Press. (Orig. pub. 1929.)

Wilson, Scott. 2001. "Carruthers and the Argument from Marginal Cases." *Journal of Applied Philosophy* 18:135–47.

Wise, Steven. 2000. *Rattling the Cage: Toward Legal Rights for Animals.* Cambridge, Mass.: Perseus Books.

Wolterstorff, Nicholas. 2008. *Justice: Rights and Wrongs.* Princeton: Princeton University Press.

Wolterstorff, Nicholas, and Robert Audi. 1997. *Religion in the Public Square.* Lanham, Md.: Rowman and Littlefield.

Yoder, John Howard. 1972. *The Politics of Jesus.* Grand Rapids, Mich.: Eerdmans.

Zafirovski, Milan. 2007. *Liberal Modernity and Its Adversaries.* Boston: Brill.

Zahn, Gordon. 1989. *German Catholics and Hitler's Wars.* Notre Dame: University of Notre Dame Press. (Orig. pub. 1962.)

Zuckert, Michael. 2002. *Launching Liberalism: On Lockean Political Philosophy.* Lawrence: University Press of Kansas.

INDEX